When Michele says journey, I sta … I know my truth-telling friend has … . I encourage you to join in and enco… …is illuminated path of discovery. And plan on camping out on her brilliant questions. I'll bring s'mores.

—Patsy Clairmont, speaker, Women of Faith/Belong;
author, *You Are More Than You Know*

Michele Cushatt has earned the right to be heard. Period. If you're looking for a couple of months' worth of platitudes, you've chosen the wrong book. Textured by Michele's physical and spiritual scars from battles you wouldn't wish on your worst enemy, *I Am* will both convict and thrill you.

—Jerry Jenkins, writer of the Left Behind series

Using vulnerable personal stories, insightful biblical teaching, and soul-searching reflection, Michele Cushatt helped me reframe my life through the lens of who God is and who I am because I am His. Through this powerful sixty-day journey, I found hope and courage to let God rewrite the story I am living and the story I am telling myself every day.

—Renee Swope, author, award-winning *A Confident Heart*

If you ever struggle as I do with the question, "Am I enough?" this book is for you. Michele didn't learn these powerful lessons from the comfort of an armchair as a spectator of the lives of others. The personal, practical wisdom she shares came from deep, dark places and will bring light and healing to all who dive in.

—Sheila Walsh, cohost, *Life Today*

On the pages of *I Am* you will find you are wanted, heard, healed, enough, safe, and that you belong. You will not close this book the same as when you started!

—Lysa TerKeurst, *New York Times* bestselling author;
president of Proverbs 31 Ministries

With an honest, compelling, and *fun* voice, Michele Cushatt invites us into a thorough understanding of who God has made and called us to be. This sixty-day read can make a difference of us, whether we're sixteen or sixty years old. Come and see yourself as God sees you!

—Elisa Morgan, speaker; author, *The Beauty of Broken* and *Hello, Beauty Full*; cohost, *Discover the Word*

Michele Cushatt is a beautiful messenger from the deep well of personal trial. I needed her words in this devotional book: to remind me of who I am and of the great I Am who changes everything. Grace and truth are found in these pages. Thank you, Michele, for this most timely word—one I will read over and over again.

—Lisa Whittle, speaker; author, *{w}hole* and *I Want God*

When life gets hard, we too easily lose sight of who we are. It seems the world screams lies at us while God whispers truth to our hearts. On the pages of this book, Michele brings a megaphone to God's voice so we can silence the lies and grab hold of the truth. Let these words soak into your soul so you can stand firm in who you really are.

—Jill Savage, founder and CEO of Hearts at Home; author, *No More Perfect Moms*

I Am

Also by Michele Cushatt

Undone: A Story of Making Peace with an Unexpected Life

I Am

A Sixty-Day Journey to Knowing Who You Are because of Who He Is

Michele Cushatt

ZONDERVAN®

ZONDERVAN

I Am

Requests for information should be addressed to:
Zondervan, *3900 Sparks Dr. SE, Grand Rapids, Michigan 49546*

ISBN 978-0-310-33980-9 (softcover)

ISBN 978-0-310-33981-6 (ebook)

Published in association with the literary agency of Wolgemuth and Associates, Inc.

Cover design: Studio Gearbox
Cover image: Shutterstock®
Interior design: Kait Lamphere

First printing November 2016 / Printed in the United States of America

20 21 PC/LSCH 10 9 8

To Loren P. Trethewey,
"Papa"
(1944–2014)

You found yourself in Him.
May I have courage to do the same.

Amen, hallelujah.
Praise the Lord.

For whoever wants to save their life will lose it,
but whoever loses their life for me will save it.

—JESUS (LUKE 9:24)

Contents

PART 1: Creation

PART 2: Exodus

PART 3: Covenant

PART 4: Presence

PART 5: Rescue

PART 6: Revelation

ACKNOWLEDGMENTS

It is said that, when asked if writing books proved a hard endeavor, Ernest Hemingway offered up this reply: “Why, no. You simply sit down at the typewriter, open your veins, and bleed.”

Search further into the history of this near-legendary quote, and you’ll discover a lengthy collection of other writers who’ve been given credit for these words. Thomas Wolfe, Red Smith, and Friedrich Nietzsche, among others.

Perhaps it doesn’t matter so much who said it first. All of us who put pen to paper feel a bit of ownership. We, more than anyone, know its truth.

I often muse how nice it would be to write books that require less—how shall I say?—*surgery*. Perhaps a donut pop-up book. A how-to manual for professional nap-taking. Or, maybe, something to do with napkin folding.

Instead, I find myself on the hunt for life-saving, life-giving words, the kind of words that require myself on an operating table, chest split open, and more than a little panic about whether I’ll come out of it alive. Let’s just say I’ve done my share of bleeding as of late.

The names that follow are those who circled up in the OR as I turned the knife on myself and searched for anything of use inside. These men and women held vigil, offered transfusions, and kept defibrillation paddles close by, just in case. A few even took their role a bit more seriously. More than once, their expert hands wielded the knife. Gently, but with precision. Seeing life hidden behind flesh, they dared to force a little bloodletting. For these precious ones, I'm eternally grateful. Not entirely happy about the lack of donuts or napkin folding, but deeply in their debt.

Carolyn. Londa. Brian. Brandon. Andrew. Joy. Ruthanne. Carla. Ken. Diane. Candie. Juli. Linda. Melissa. Lisa. Anne. Cheri. Patsy. Crystal. Renee. Kathi. Rhonda. Lindsey. Becky. Robbie. Kay. Kris. Nathan. Yvette. Tangie. Janice. Susan. Kate. Troy.

"Wounds from a friend can be trusted," Proverbs 27:6 says.

Yes, they can.

Introduction

In Search of Enough

Take off your sandals, for the place where you are standing is holy ground.
—The I am to Moses (Ex. 3:5)

He left it on the kitchen table where I sit every morning nursing my cup of coffee.

"It's starry night," he announced.

I looked with a vague sense of familiarity at his crayon sketch.

"Starry night," he said again.

That's when I knew. *The* Starry Night. As in the famous painting housed in New York City's Museum of Modern Art.

Well, then. Impressive. My third-grade boy not only had created a fine replica of a famous art piece, he also knew its title.

"Do you know who painted it?"

"Venison van Gogh."

I stifled a laugh.

Simple and sweet, drawn as only an eight-year-old can. I *loved* it. It would never grace the walls of a museum or gallery. It would be measured by a mother's affection alone, not by the one-hundred-million-dollar value of van Gogh's masterpiece.

It's not the medium that lends value to a piece of work. It's the artist.

Personal identity and value have become wildly popular. We've always been preoccupied with self, but we're also highly self-aware. Not only do we spend time and money to better understand ourselves, but we've also made self-celebration a priority.

This isn't necessarily a bad thing. Whether we're eight years old or eighty, we want to know we are valued by those we love.

Followers of Christ speak into this self-aware culture with different perspectives. One of the most popular powerfully promises that what you speak will come true.

Wake up every day and say, "I am beautiful," and beauty will come to you.

Or speak, "I am financially successful," and wealth will come your way.

Or declare, "I am healthy and strong," and healing will overcome any injury or disease.

The promise: we control our destinies. Therefore, we need to own our identities and call our best selves out. Then we'll get the lives we've always dreamed of. After all, God wants us to be happy, right?

While positivity and self-affirmation have their places, this promise is flawed.

Worse, it's dangerous.

I'll get to that, but first, I need to tell you a story. My story.

It started with a phone call.

Tuesday morning. Two days before Thanksgiving. Moments before, I'd sent my three boys off to school. My husband was headed to work, and I planned to spend the day grocery shopping for friends and relatives who were soon to arrive.

But on the phone the doctor said cancer.

I was thirty-nine years old and I had squamous-cell carcinoma of the tongue. I hadn't even known such a thing existed.

What followed were weeks and months of doctor's appointments, PET scans, and a painful surgery to remove a small section of my tongue. Cancer caught early, the doctors told me. Relieved, I recovered, we packed up cancer, put it on a shelf, and expected never to see it again.

Until it came back. Twice. Three years later, and again eight months after that.

No more smiling doctors and promises of a cure. No more putting cancer on a shelf. Instead, a nine-hour operation—again two days before Thanksgiving—followed by two months of chemotherapy and radiation.

My doctors said they threw everything at it but the kitchen sink, desperate to give me the best chance at a long life. In the process, I nearly died.

That I didn't die was celebrated as a miracle by friends and family, but I struggled. Survival proved costly.

I'd become unrecognizable. Two scars on my neck evidenced the removal of lymph nodes and blood vessels. I'd lost two-thirds of my tongue, including function and taste. Surgeons used tissue and vessels from my left arm to rebuild my tongue. My left leg sported a scar the size of an iPhone 6, where surgeons had removed flesh to rebuild my left arm. Radiation burns covered my face, neck, and chest, and painful ulcers filled my lips, mouth, and throat. For six weeks, I had a tracheostomy, and for five months, a feeding tube.

I would never look, speak, or eat the same again.

Emotional and spiritual ravaging left me with far deeper scars.

If you had asked me five years before—or even one year before—whether my identity and self-worth were based on my appearance, my talents, and my career, I would have said, "Absolutely not!"

Ask me that question today.

This happens to us all at some point. A crisis hits like a storm. Divorce. Death. Loss. Our stories differ, but the fallout is the same: we lose sight of who we are.

We become unrecognizable. And so we struggle to regain our footing, to find our place, to feel secure in who we are.

But no matter how we grab for a sense of significance, it remains out of reach. We're not sure who we are anymore, and we haven't a clue where to find the answer.

~

Enter Moses.

I've long had an affinity with the patriarch of Exodus. Maybe because of his complicated young adulthood, his powerful emotions, and his radical midlife career change.

Like mine, Moses' world changed with a call. Unlike mine, his came from a burning bush. A *talking*, burning bush. Check out Exodus chapter three.

"Moses! Moses!" a voice spoke from the flames (v. 4).

Somehow, even without experience with talking shrubbery, Moses knew to answer, "Here I am."

"I have indeed seen the misery of my people in Egypt," said the voice. "I have heard them crying out because of their slave drivers, and I am concerned about their suffering" (v. 7).

I imagine Moses nodding, taking it all in. *Great. Fabulous. About time. Not sure what this has to do with me, though.*

As if sensing his confusion, the voice clears things up: "So now, go. I am sending you to Pharaoh to bring my people the Israelites out of Egypt" (v. 10).

Wait, wha?! With all due respect, Holy One of the Hot Bush, have you lost your ever-loving mind?

Okay, so maybe those weren't Moses' exact words. But he quickly cataloged all the reasons why he wasn't the right guy for the job. His Israelite ancestry. His adoptive evil Pharaoh father. His moment of explosive anger and murder. His unsavory exit, followed by his forty-year shepherding exile. His lack of experience. His lack of a shower.

"Who am I that I should go to Pharaoh and bring the Israelites out of Egypt?" (v. 11).

Who am I?

Moses' burning question. And the question we all ask.

Who am I to do this hard thing?

Who am I to be chosen?

Who am I to be loved?

Who am I? Really?

I have a shady family history, you might say. I'm not attractive, educated, or talented. Heck, I can't even get my kids to school on time or love my husband without wanting to drop kick them all to Texas.

My apologies to Texas.

I understand. I really do. Most mornings I wake up determined to try harder, to be better, to work with the passion of someone who knows how much it all matters.

But good intentions give way to real life, usually before lunch.

Who am I? I'm afraid I already know the answer.

For some of us, our doubt is as obvious as Moses' burning bush. We make too many mistakes, bear too many flaws, harbor too many regrets. God may love the next guy. But not us. Definitely not us.

Some of us keep hearing the echoes of those who said we'd never amount to anything. Whoever it was—parent, spouse, teacher, friend—their criticisms are pressed into our memory like handprints in cement. Even if the person is long gone, the hurt continues to haunt.

Or maybe your biggest critic is you, and you can't seem to stop the way you feel about yourself, the way you talk to yourself.

You rear-end someone. *I'm such an idiot.*

You snap at your children. *I'm a terrible parent.*

You show up late—again. *What's wrong with me? Will I ever get this right?*

No amount of affirmation or encouragement seems to stick. Like a file cabinet filled with bills you can't pay, your mind bulges with accusations. You wish you were someone other than who you are.

Who am I?

Moses stands barefoot at a burning bush. He asks his question. Then, along with us, waits for an answer.

But God's two-part response isn't at all what we expect.

"I will be with you," He says (v. 12).

Nothing about Moses' skills or abilities; nothing about Moses at all.

Just assurance.

But Moses pushes for more.

"Suppose I go to the Israelites and say to them, 'The God of your fathers has sent me to you,' and they ask me, 'What is his name?' Then what shall I tell them?" (v. 13).

I need credibility, and we both know I don't have it. So at least send me with a solid reference.

God does exactly that: "This is what you are to say to the Israelites: 'I AM has sent me to you'" (v. 14).

Not a list of Moses' merits. Not a glowing recommendation of his speaking skills or relational talents. Instead, God's own unspeakable name. The four letters of the tetragrammaton, the Hebrew name for God. Devout Jews wouldn't say it or write it without holy preparation.

Obviously, the ultimate endorsement for Moses.

So what does this have to do with us?

Everything.

To Moses' burning question—and to ours—God delivers a two-part answer:

- Presence. *I will be with you.*
- Purpose. *I AM sending you.*

One assures us we're not alone. The other reminds us we're chosen by the only one qualified to choose.

Identity isn't grounded in who we are; it's grounded in who He is.

We've bought the notion that our worth has something to do with us. That if we want to be smart and strong and beautiful and successful, we need to call ourselves out, speak into our own greatness.

But the calling is God's, not ours.

Who am I? God says He's the one who gets to decide. Not the critic who nitpicks our every move. Not the parent who's never pleased or the spouse who can't see beyond the conflict. Not even us, as we vacillate between self-loathing and self-adulation. Only the Creator can assign value to His creation. And throughout the Bible, verse after verse, God tells us exactly how He feels about who we are:

- "You are precious and honored in my sight, and because I love you" (Isa. 43:4).
- "You are worth more than many sparrows" (Matt. 10:31).
- "I have engraved you on the palms of my hands" (Isa. 49:16).

Holy ground. Burning with sacred, inextinguishable truth.

We mustn't forget: our best efforts are still childlike replicas of a greater work. Beautiful, yes. But limited. Rather than agonizing over our lack of self-worth, we can anchor ourselves to the unfathomable value of being an original work. A masterpiece created by the Master for the display of His incredible glory.

Jesus couldn't have made it clearer: "Whoever finds their life will lose it, and whoever loses their life for my sake will find it" (Matt. 10:39). Only when we allow ourselves to be swallowed by His greatness do we discover our unshakeable place in this world.

Timothy Keller, in his book *The Reason for God*, says it this way: "If anything threatens your identity, you will not just be anxious but paralyzed with fear. If you lose your identity through the failings of someone else, you will not just be resentful but locked into bitterness. If you lose it through your own failings, you will hate or despise yourself as a failure as long as you live. Only if your identity is built on God and his love . . . can you have a self that can venture anything, face anything."[1]

It's not about what you and I call out. It's about wearing the name we've already been given. We bring nothing to the table. He brings everything.

As you and I begin this sixty-day trek together, you need to know a few important details. First, this book is divided into six parts: "Creation," "Exodus," "Covenant," "Presence," "Rescue," and "Revelation." Think of each as a key piece of the overall story of the Bible. You and I are characters in a grand narrative far more glorious than our small, individual ones. When we finally grasp the wonder of this, and then embrace our unique role in the story, we'll experience a security we've never before known.

Second, each day begins with a verse from the Bible in which God speaks directly about His children—us. These are designed to root out and replace the many lesser messages you and I have listened to for far too long. Let His words soak deep into your soul.

Still, not every verse and truth is easy. Yes, many days we'll bask in God's beautiful assurances. We are chosen, loved, rescued, honored. These are balms to our bruised souls. But building identity on truth means receiving the hard words as well, the truths that sting but ultimately set us free. We are sinful, proud, needy, lost. Understanding our unworthiness frees us to embrace God's incredible worth and, as a result, our incomparable worth in Him. As pastor and teacher John Piper says, "Our passionate preference for Jesus' worth is our worth. Our preference, embrace, treasuring of Jesus as supremely valuable is my value . . . Therefore, woven into your worthiness is a profound sense of unworthiness."[2]

Finally, at the end of each day's journey is a section titled "Who am I?" Habits are hard to break, especially deep-seated emotional ones. "Who am I?" is designed to move us past head knowledge to change our core beliefs. The questions dive deeper, push harder. Press through, my friend. The greatest transformation comes through discomfort. My greatest hope is that when you and I arrive at the end of this journey, we'll be men and women who stand tall in the knowledge of who we truly are. Not because we have called ourselves out but because He has.

When it comes to Moses' burning question, you and I can exhale. The pressure is off. It's not up to us to be worthy; it's on God. He's the Savior. The Artist. The wielder of paint and brush in your life. And His work is worth far more than a mere hundred million.

So slip off your shoes. You're stepping onto holy ground.

I am with you, He says.

I have chosen you, He reassures.

He is—so you are—enough.

Part 1

CREATION

Day 1

I Am Created

It is I who made the earth and created mankind on it. My own hands stretched out the heavens; I marshaled their starry hosts.

—Isaiah 45:12

It was the summer before my fifteenth birthday.

As they did every summer, Mom and Dad packed my younger brother and me into our family car, hitched the pop-up camper, and set out from Illinois on our annual family vacation.

Usually we turned toward Minnesota to lose ourselves in fishing and swimming (and mosquito swatting) at one of the state's ten thousand lakes. This year we traveled halfway across the country to Wyoming, a place I'd never been before. There we met my grandparents and explored Grand Teton and Yellowstone national parks together.

In a childhood filled with family vacations, I can't remember every sight and sound my younger self experienced. There were too many vacations, too many memories to savor and store. But one moment during that 1986 vacation I'll never forget: the moment I stood on the shore of Jenny Lake.

Located in the upper northwest corner of Wyoming, Jenny Lake is an oval body of pristine water nestled at the base of the Grand Teton mountain range. The lake is not very big, less than a square two miles, dwarfed by the towering peaks of the Grand Tetons. But what Jenny Lake lacks in size it makes up for in beauty.

Geologists believe that thousands of years ago, during the Ice Age, glaciers traveled down the canyons to carve out deep depressions in the valley floor. Then water filled the depressions—more than 250-feet deep—creating a lake clear as crystal against the backdrop of towering, craggy mountains. The result is stunning.

My fifteen-year-old self stood on the shore of this natural phenomenon and could scarcely breathe. Even now, I remember the way my soul soaked up the moment. If other tourists shared my shore, I didn't notice. With the sun on my back and the scenery spread out before me, I stood entranced. Overcome. I was being wooed by glory.

This midwestern flatland girl didn't know what to do with such a scene. It was otherworldly. I knew it wasn't the mountains and waters inviting my awe but the Creator of both. It was as if God stood at my right side, arm draped over a shoulder, and whispered into my ear, "I made that, my girl. I made it for you."

Geologists may claim nature created Jenny Lake. But I knew better. Still do. From my early days in itty-bitty Sunday school chairs, teachers told me, "In the beginning, God created" (Gen. 1:1). And I believed it. Five words that sum up the source of everything. Oceans. Stars. Crawdads. Eagles. Fruit flies.

(For the record, my bananas could've done without the last one.)

In the beginning, God created. As if it were as simple as "in the beginning, God made a ham sandwich." Because God wanted to. And because God could. That includes the Grand Tetons and Jenny Lake.

It also includes me.

This last part proved harder to accept, both at fifteen years old and at forty-four. I could see the creative genius of a mountain range. But prop me next to the Tetons and I could hardly compare. My hair was too thin, my teeth too crooked, and my personality too strong. I wasn't majestic or captivating. Not even close. When it came to God's creative capacity, Jenny Lake was stunning. But me? I felt like an accident of nature rather than a marvel of creation.

And yet I couldn't deny God's words penned in Genesis. Humankind is the pinnacle of His creation. *Me.* If I was to build my identity on truth, I needed to begin where it all begins. With creation.

Genesis means "origin" or "beginning," and the book of Genesis answers the great questions behind all questions: Where do I come from? And why am I here? Genesis provides us with roots. Those powerful, winding, digging legs a tree sends into the ground to hold it firmly in place.

So why is it so hard to grasp? Why do you and I struggle to see ourselves as marvelous creations of an artistic God?

Perhaps because we're too caught up in the flaws to be captivated by the glory.

Maybe a return to Jenny Lake could help. Think about it this way: Jenny Lake didn't begin as a lake. She began as a smooth valley floor until glaciers carved up her space. It took hardship and hundreds of years for Jenny Lake to show a greater glory. That too was part of God's creative plan.

This means you and I, with all our hardships and imperfections, are still held in the hand of a sovereign and creative God. He created us, and He is creating us still. He isn't done yet, and He always finishes what He starts.

Philippians 1:6 says it this way: "Being confident of this, that he who began a good work in you will carry it on to completion until the day of Christ Jesus."

That means that the God who created us will also complete us. This is the bedrock we've long been looking for, the cement for the rest of our stories: "For everything God created is good" (1 Tim. 4:4).

When you and I look in the mirror and struggle to see evidence of a marvelous creation, it's simply because we're catching a glimpse of a work in progress. But in spite of our many flaws, we remain a creation of a masterful God who has nothing but affection for His work of art and anticipates its completion.

You.

Stand on the shore and marvel at what He's done. What He *is doing*. Allow yourself to be wooed by glory. And if you quiet yourself just enough, you might hear Him whisper in your ear, "I made you, dear child. I made *you*."

You never know what may cause them. The sight of the Atlantic Ocean can do it, or a piece of music, or a face you've never seen before. A pair of somebody's old shoes can do it. . . . You can never be sure. But of this you can be sure. Whenever you find tears in your eyes, especially unexpected tears, it is well to pay the closest attention. They are not only telling you something about the secret of who you are, but more often than not God is speaking to you through them of the mystery of where you have come from and is summoning you to where you should go to next.

—Frederick Buechner, *Whistling in the Dark*

Who Am I?

What we believe about our origin has a significant impact on the value we ascribe to ourselves. If I believe I'm an accident of nature, my sense of identity will reflect that belief. But if I believe I've been crafted by the Creator, I can accept I'm of infinite artistic worth, made by the hands of a genius. Like me, you may have far more questions than answers when it comes to your origin and the creation of this world. For today, stand and look with wonder upon your unique life. Like that midwestern girl at the base of the Grand Tetons, take in the view with renewed appreciation of the Creator's marvelous work.

Day 2

I Am Formed

Everyone who is called by my name, whom I created for my glory, whom I formed and made.

Isaiah 43:7

I cringe every time I see it.

My first-grade school photo.

Dorothy Hamill haircut. Awkward 1970s fashion. Slouchy shoulders, goofy grin. And a gap between my two front teeth as wide as Moses' parted Red Sea.

Somebody save me.

I always hated that gap. Lauren Hutton made it look sexy. I made it look like an unfortunate genetic accident. For two entire school years that photo bothered my six-year-old self. So much so that it affected my third- and fourth-grade photos.

Again, Dorothy hair. Still no clue about posture. But my lips are tightly pressed together, hiding my Red Sea pearly whites. Effective, yes. But it left me looking like I suffered digestive issues.

I inherited my toothy space. Call it a genetic gift, passed down from my mother's side of the family, along with a wide and sturdy Nebraska-farmer physique.

Yay me.

But unlike the Nebraska hips, which I didn't resent until much later, I hated my teeth from the start. They made me different. Other six-year-olds sported teeth that touched. Mine had to send postcards to each other. I tried to squish them together with my fingers to no avail. Mom tried to convince me the gap made me unique. I didn't want to be unique. I wanted to be normal.

That was merely the beginning of an ongoing personal critique that continues to this day. Imagine me, clipboard in hand, constantly scrutinizing my reflection.

Turned-up nose? Check.

Wrinkles and flabby granny arms? Check, check.

Gray hair, spider veins, and stretch marks? Lord, have mercy. Somebody give me a fresh pen. Check, check, and *check*.

When it comes to my appearance, there is far too little I celebrate and far too much I denigrate. But if my little girl came up to me and started the same type of clipboard-carrying critique, I'd grab her by the shoulders and launch into a world-class lecture detailing all the reasons why she is beautiful and wonderful and valuable exactly as she is.

Why can't I do the same for myself?

Because I've lost sight of how I was formed. In my effort to be like everyone else, I've lost sight of what makes me one of a kind. Just as there's a painter behind every painting and a poet behind every poem, an artistic expertise forged every one of us. And the best artists know that variation lends creativity its value. It isn't the common that attracts us but the uncommon.

Years ago, long before his explosive success, my parents became fans of artist Terry Redlin. They loved his outdoor wildlife scenes, the way he brought nature alive with color and illumination. So one day they picked up a Terry Redlin print. But not just any print. A numbered print—one of a limited edition of original paintings. Replicas of that painting exist, but none exactly like theirs. Theirs includes variations not found in the replicas, unique brush strokes that lend originality to their particular piece of art.

What if you and I started to see our variations the same way? What if, rather than conforming to a standard, working so hard to become a mass-produced replica, we trusted the value in the unique form we already have?

What if your curly hair is actually like a numbered print?

What if that birthmark or those freckles you try to hide are like a signature?

What if my cavernous front teeth are like an artist's hidden representation?

To the believers in Ephesus, Paul wrote these words: "For we are God's handiwork, created in Christ Jesus to do good works, which God prepared in advance for us to do" (Eph. 2:10).

In the original text, Paul's word for handiwork is *polema*, the Greek word from which we get poem. But the best part comes in the word right after handiwork.

Created. From *ktizo*, "to design with a certain ability, capability, or capacity."[3]

Did you see that? *To design.* Design takes creation to the next level, conveying the intention, purpose, and skill of the Designer, expertise commissioned to do an expert task.

We are not mass produced, like millions of candies poured into molds and coming out exactly the same as all the others.

We've been designed by an expert, shaped and formed by hands with far more skill than our own. Given life, then crafted into the best possible representation of the Artist. We were formed, uniquely and individually, with qualities both external and internal that make us unlike any other.

Numbered prints. Each one different from all the others. Each one bearing the name of the Artist. Gap teeth and all.

Day 2

The church is an orchestra. We are instruments crafted by the Artist. We play a score written for us by the Composer, which allows our individual notes to create harmonies. Having tuned ourselves to the Perfect Pitch living within, we play as one, interpreting the Composer's masterpiece with passion and precision. And the result is stunning: we display the glory of God.

—Charles R. Swindoll, *Insights on Romans*

Who Am I?

A recent report claimed that a massive seven billion dollars is spent every year on cosmetics, not to mention cosmetic surgeries, clothing, and athletic gear.[4] If we don't like how we look, we spare little expense to fix it. Consider for a moment this culture of dissatisfaction. How has it influenced the way you see yourself and how you spend your time and money? There's nothing wrong with highlighting your hair, buying a nice jacket, or putting on some mascara. But where do we draw the line between self-care and obsessive self-modification? In your efforts to fit in, have you lost something of your unique form?

Day 3

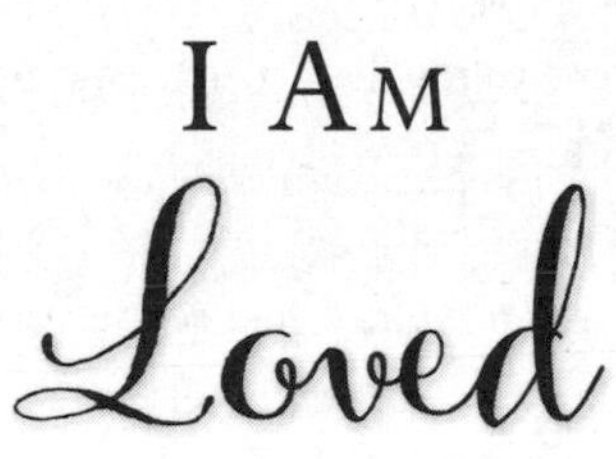

I have loved you with an everlasting love.

—Jeremiah 31:3

A glance at the old digital clock made me want to scream.

5:50 a.m.

On a Saturday. For the love.

Can't a girl catch a break? You should know I'm a hardcore morning person. Most days I'm up no later than 6:00 a.m. In a house filled with children who seldom stop moving or talking, it's my only real shot at peace and quiet.

Feel free to shout amen. Or send espresso.

But it was the weekend, and I needed a break. For two weeks I'd poured myself into loving my family. Meal preparation, homework, endless errands and grocery shopping, and four always-talking, always-moving children.

Like a blistering stretch of heat-filled days, exhaustion had turned me dry and brittle. I desperately needed sleep, extra quiet minutes snuggled under the sheets, time to rest, and space to breathe. I needed someone to fill up the love I'd been pouring out.

It was not to be. I was awake, no matter how much I didn't want to be.

Day 3

With a groan, I slid from the sheets, careful not to wake my snoring spouse. In silence, I dressed, closed the bedroom door, and made my way downstairs.

I paused in the foyer, next to the double French doors leading into my office. I had work to do, always more work to do. A never-ending pile of to-do's pulled me to my desk. But in spite of my never-assuaged guilt, I knew I had nothing left to give.

So I grabbed coffee, journal, and Bible and seated myself outside.

For more than thirty minutes I just sat and stared at the dark gray morning sky. Too weary to do anything else.

God, I need you. I'm empty.

It happened so fast I would have missed it had I stepped inside for a coffee refill. One moment the sky appeared shades of purple, the next moment as if someone had struck a match and set the sky on fire in hues of pink and orange. Though the temperature remained chilly, I felt heat, as if the sun's reflection off the clouds were a fireplace burning in the morning sky.

Like a message meant for me, a jumble of familiar words filled my mind, warming my soul as the sun showed off:

> *I wait for the Lord, my whole being waits,*
> *and in his word, I put my hope.*
> *I wait for the Lord*
> *more than watchmen wait for the morning,*
> *more than watchmen wait for the morning.*
> *Israel, put your hope in the Lord,*
> *for with the Lord is unfailing love*
> *and with him is full redemption.*
> *He himself will redeem Israel*
> *from all their sins.*
>
> —Psalm 130:5–8

For with the Lord is unfailing love.

Unfailing love. The kind that doesn't give out. The kind that isn't reluctant to embrace my empty self. The kind that can fill a bankrupt mama with enough to get her through another day.

The sunrise almost over, another message came to mind.

> *Because of the* Lord*'s great love we are not consumed,*
> *for his compassions never fail.*
> *They are new every morning;*
> *great is your faithfulness.*
> *I say to myself, "The* Lord *is my portion;*
> *therefore I will wait for him."*
>
> —Lamentations 3:22–24

Because of the Lord*'s great love we are not consumed.*

I soaked up those words like the sun's warming rays in the cool of morning.

For the two weeks prior, I'd felt consumed. Consumed by responsibility. Consumed by weariness. Consumed by this never-slowing life that requires more from me than I can give. Sometimes being a wife, mom, and business owner isn't what I dreamed it to be. It involves far more giving than receiving, far more loving than being loved. If I hired an accountant to keep tabs on my heart, he'd find me in the red more often than not. I can see it in the dark circles under my eyes and hear it in my oft-curt replies.

But as I watched the sun take its place in the sky, as I savored the unexpected gift of an ordinary morning, I realized something: It isn't lazy Saturday mornings that sustain me; it's God's incomparable, unfailing love. A love He delights to deliver through an unexpected Saturday morning sunrise.

Within minutes of the sunrise's end, I found the connection between these two seemingly random Bible passages that God had so clearly brought to mind. I found it in the words "unfailing love" (Ps. 130:7) and "great love" (Lam. 3:24). With a quick word study I discovered them to be the same Hebrew word: *hesed.*

One of the most important words of the entire Old Testament. A word that means "love, kindness, mercy." It's a kindness "reserved for close friends and family members . . . An act of *hesed* presupposed the existence of a relationship between the parties involved, but where no formal relationship has previously been recognized, the person exercising *hesed* has chosen to treat the recipient as if such a relationship did exist."[5]

Did you get that? *Hesed*—God's *hesed*—is not dependent on us. It's not about doing more or being more. It's not about sleeping in or waking early, working in the wee hours or journaling on the deck. I could've slept in rather than read the Psalms, and God's love for me wouldn't have been any greater.

Firm, steadfast, unfailing . . . mercy, kindness, and love.

Hesed.

It's not about us; it's about Him. And we are loved.

We can be humble only when we know that we are God's children, of infinite value, and eternally loved.

—Madeleine L'Engle, *Walking on Water*

Who Am I?

How loved do you feel on a scale of 1 to 10 (10 being infinitely and perfectly loved)? According to the truth of the Bible, God's love for you is a perfect 10. But rarely do we feel that way. What's getting in the way of your receiving that kind of love? Be specific, writing your thoughts in a journal or in the margin. Then read Psalm 136 and soak up God's *hesed*—His infinite love, mercy, and kindness—for you.

Day 4

I Am Beautiful

Do not consider his appearance or his height, for I have rejected him. The Lord does not look at the things people look at. People look at the outward appearance, but the Lord looks at the heart.

—1 Samuel 16:7

His name was, let's say, Mark.

We were both sophomores at a Christian college in the Midwest. I didn't know him well, although on a small campus such as ours, everyone knew everyone. Drop eight hundred students in overpopulated dorms and intimate classrooms, and it doesn't take long for each of us to know who had sneaked out the night before and what family drama we'd left behind at home.

Mark wasn't notable. Mildly attractive and well liked, connected to all the other attractive and well-liked people. Even in college, the high school hierarchy continued.

I'd planned to go to medical school. But a come-to-Jesus altar call at a high school youth conference changed my trajectory. I wanted to go overseas, help the needy, tell people about Jesus. So I abandoned medicine and enrolled at a Christian college, dreaming of Africa or Russia or some other place where I would change the world.

Instead, my world changed.

It happened a few weeks before Christmas break. Although I'd been in college for three semesters, I still struggled to find my place. I had great grades, plenty of friends. But the "freshman fifteen" turned out to be no joke, and I'd gained my full share of allotted pounds. If my self-perception hadn't already been skewed, I might've been able to accept my new physique, maybe take the necessary steps to change it. But for as long as I could remember, I'd never liked my appearance. Adding fifteen pounds to it only deepened my self-disgust.

This was the status of my self-esteem on the afternoon I overheard a male voice coming around a hallway corner: "Take Michele, for example."

At the sound of my name, I stopped. Held my breath.

The voice—which I recognized as Mark's—continued.

"She's one of those who'd be beautiful if she wasn't so fat. Know what I mean?"

I couldn't move.

I don't know what he said next, didn't stick around long enough to find out. Humiliated, I found my legs, ran to my dorm room, and wept.

Several days later, I confronted Mark, let him know I'd overheard his comments outside the cafeteria. His face reddened—as it should have—but he fell short of apologizing. His only offering: "I meant it as a compliment!"

Weeks later, the semester finished, I packed my college dorm room, loaded up my car, and moved back home.

I never returned. My broken and humiliated heart couldn't risk another beating.

A part of me still wants to blame Mark, maybe even hate him. I can still feel the sting, can well remember the lingering shame. A compliment? Really? With a few careless words, he caused damage that took years to heal.

But I don't hate him. Or blame him. Mark was a nineteen-year-old *kid*. He probably still took his laundry home to his mama on the weekends. And although his words hurt, they simply confirmed what I'd long believed: beautiful was out of reach for me.

I'm now forty-four years old. I have six children and a husband and wear a size eight(ish). But in the past two decades, I've been everything from a size two to an eighteen. At each size, regardless of how big or small, I didn't see myself as beautiful. Whether I passed a bathroom mirror or caught a glimpse of myself in a store window's glass, I still heard the same words: "You'd be beautiful if . . ."

You see, beautiful isn't about size. Nor is it about Mark. It's about how I see *me*. And what I choose to believe as a result.

We all want to feel beautiful, attractive, or desirable in some small way. It's human. But somewhere along the way, we bought into a voice that puts beautiful out of reach. Doesn't matter if it was a boyfriend, a teacher, a neighbor, or yourself. Then and now, the voice is loud. As a result, when we see a reflection or a photo, we don't see beautiful. We cringe and believe a lie: "I'd be beautiful if . . ."

What if there's a better definition of beauty?

In the Old Testament, there's a story about a prophet named Samuel, whom God chooses to appoint a new king. There's an assumption that the king needs to be tall, strong, and attractive. Look the part. Kingly. And yet when God sees a parade of premier choices, He shakes His head at every one: "Do not consider his appearance or his height, for I have rejected him. The LORD does not look at the things people look at. People look at the outward appearance, but the LORD looks at the heart" (1 Sam. 16:7).

Ouch. God isn't the one who puts a premium on appearance. We are. Height. Weight. Hair color. Clothing style. We're addicted to beauty, drawn to beautiful things like moths to a light. Our mistake isn't in the appreciation of beauty; it's in the assumption that beauty equals worth. And that beauty equals love.

God says we couldn't be more wrong. Consider Isaiah's description of Jesus, the Messiah: "He had no beauty or majesty to attract us to him, nothing in his appearance that we should desire him. He was despised and rejected" (Isa. 53:2–3).

Jesus. God's one and only. Anything but beautiful. A man people would defame and whisper about in hallways and around corners. Ultimately, a man persecuted and destroyed.

And yet a man who couldn't have been more precious to the Father.

It is said that beauty is in the eye of the beholder. But too often, we choose the wrong beholder—ourselves and others, flawed beings who can't see clearly. Only God has perfect vision, seeing beyond the false exterior to the authentic heart. And when He looks at you, He sees an unmatched creation, someone He loves enough to die for.

So what does God see as beautiful?

Beautiful is giving your life for another.

Beautiful is comforting those who hurt.

Beautiful is finding joy in the ordinary of each day.

Beautiful is believing God is with us, even when we feel alone.

Beautiful is cheering for those who struggle, and helping them finish their race.

Beautiful is seeing the best in others.

Beautiful is humility.

Beautiful is perseverance.

Beautiful is generosity.

Beautiful is knowing you're beautiful, believing you're beautiful, because the one who sees the real you better than anyone else says so.

Beautiful.

Is.

You.

People travel to wonder at the height of mountains, at the huge waves of the sea, at the long courses of rivers, at the vast compass of the ocean, at the circular motion of the stars; and they pass by themselves without wondering . . . Now, let us acknowledge the wonder of our physical incarnation—that we are here, in these particular bodies, at this particular time, in these particular circumstances. May we never take for granted the gift of our individuality.

—St. Augustine, *Confessions*

Who Am I?

Beauty is a powerful part of our culture, such that it's difficult to change our perceptions and definitions of it. It's one thing to read the truth, another to *know* it. Spend a few moments thinking about the many ways you are beautiful. Think beyond the color of your eyes and the size of your clothes. Remember God's words to Samuel: "People look at the outward appearance, but the Lord looks at the heart." Here's a prayer to get you started: *God, open my eyes to see what You see when You look at me. I struggle to see myself as beautiful, but I don't want to continue that way. Affirm me with Your love, strengthen me with Your unfailing affection.*

Day 5

I Am Chosen

You did not choose me, but I chose you and appointed you so that you might go and bear fruit—fruit that will last—and so that whatever you ask in my name the Father will give you.

—John 15:16

It started on Mother's Day 2006, when my husband, Troy, handed me a wrapped gift.

"Open it," he urged.

I could see anticipation in his eyes. This was not a Mother's Day blender.

I ripped the paper from the package and almost fell out of my chair.

A laptop.

No more fighting over the family desktop. No more squeezing out a few sentences in between all the homework and bookkeeping.

No more waiting to dream.

"I want you to write," he said, eyes shining. "Anywhere you want. Anytime you want."

Tears. Rivers of them. For one of the few times in my life, I felt understood. He knew writing mattered to me, made me feel alive. He knew and wanted to help me fly.

Within months, I met with success, getting my first two submitted articles published in well-known print magazines. An unheard of scenario for a rookie, leading me to believe I'd skip over the excruciating publishing process I'd heard so much about.

I was mistaken. In the years that followed, I pushed out query after query, only to receive rejection after rejection. I agonized over proposals, only to get a "pass." I read books, attended conferences, asked questions, made changes. All while trying to be a devoted wife, mother, and employee. Life swirled, making me dizzy with the spin of it. And I wondered whether I'd need to let the writing dream die. How would I—could I—navigate all my competing roles? The tension between the responsibility and the dream was too much.

Cheered by believing family and friends, I continued, hoping maybe the Father who ordained all things had also chosen me for them. That maybe the writing was, also, a piece of His plan. So I wrote. Agonized over another book proposal. Prayed, wrestled, stayed up late at night and woke up early. Squeezed out words from sparse minutes in the hope the effort would prove worth it. And then I submitted it.

This is it! This would be my moment, I was sure of it!

And I believed that right up until the afternoon I received yet another rejection.

This time it came in email form, including a blunt critique of what I believed was my best work. This rejection made the long line of others read like compliments. I knew it was part of the process, that I should welcome the feedback. But still. My heart hurt.

As I sank to the floor in a corner of my bedroom, I began to cry. I could see my husband's bright eyes years before as I unwrapped that laptop. I could see the young woman who believed in her dream and thought she had what it takes.

That day on the bedroom floor, I felt like I failed them both.

Nothing stings quite like rejection. All the striving and believing and hoping to be chosen, only to be dashed in the trying.

Day 5

Overlooked by a parent. Passed over for a dream job. Excluded from a group of friends. Abandoned by a spouse. You always remember your greatest rejection. It becomes a demarcation point, after which something changes within. Regardless of the source, our response to rejection is often the same: self-blame.

This is our knee-jerk response to rejection. We assume we somehow aren't good enough, smart enough, worthy enough for the choosing. It's much easier to believe the deficiency lies with us, because then we might be able to fix the problem. To be at the mercy of someone else's prerogative leaves us vulnerable to further pain.

Thank heavens, God operates by a different standard. He doesn't hold back approval as He waits to evaluate our work. Instead, He has already chosen. And we made the list.

- "He will never leave you nor forsake you. Do not be afraid; do not be discouraged" (Deut. 31:8).
- "But we ought always to thank God for you, brothers loved by the Lord, because God chose you as firstfruits to be saved through the sanctifying work of the Spirit and through belief in the truth" (2 Thess. 2:13).
- "For he chose us in him before the creation of the world to be holy and blameless in his sight" (Eph. 1:4).
- And the grand finale—John's recollection of Jesus' actual words: "You did not choose me, but I chose you" (John 15:16).

Have more beautiful words ever been spoken? We're the chosen ones! We, with our many physical limitations and emotional flaws. We, with our long string of human rejections that's left us bristling and afraid. God looks at our bruised, less-than selves and sees someone worthy of love. And His choosing relieves the sting of our rejections.

Her. The second from the right. I want her. With Me.

No chance of rejection. Instead, chosen. Wanted. Celebrated. This day and every day yet to come.

Your faith is not the basis of God's choosing you, but the result of it.
—John Piper, "Ten Reasons to Revel in Being Chosen"

Who Am I?

Think of a time when you were overlooked or rejected. What was your response? Defensiveness? Indifference? Criticism? Self-blame? Now consider God's choosing of you. Picture yourself standing next to Him, handpicked to be on His team, with Him, forever. A position that cannot be changed or taken away. Can you allow this reality to take a bigger role than your rejections?

Day 6

I Am Valuable

So don't be afraid; you are worth more than many sparrows.

—*Matthew 10:31*

I'm convinced I came out of my mama's womb on the hunt for affirmation. With a hearty squawk, I poked my head out of the birth canal, raised an eyebrow, and said, "Did you see what I just did?!"

Okay, maybe not. But I've long been honing my people-pleasing skills. For too many years, it was as if I had an internal radar device always sweeping the room to gather feedback. I felt it my duty to make everyone around me happy. All the time.

It's not that I needed applause. I needed to know that I mattered, that my presence was noticed and my contributions were valued. As a young girl, this looked like a bad case of boy-crazy, combined with both flirty and fickle attempts to garner equally flirty and fickle attention. By my early twenties, it looked like tireless service to the church, spending long days and equally long nights striving to make a difference. Once I married and became a mom, my drive to please took the form of obsessive mom and control-freak wife. Effective? Hardly.

Trying to make the world happy is a wearying pursuit, to be sure. Like shooting at a moving target, I could make a person proud one day and disappointed the next.

Still, I kept trying, my radar on the lookout for someone I needed to woo, impress, or satisfy. It became an obsession. I tried to determine whether my friend's quiet demeanor meant I'd done something wrong. I wondered whether my outfit or hair or size was the reason I felt rejected. I feared my lack of intellect or charm had caused a business opportunity to pass by.

Like a hamster on a fast wheel to nowhere, I'd willingly climbed on the never-ending pursuit of perfection. A dizzying, exhausting trap.

After years of captivity, I'd had enough. It may have taken too long, but Jesus' words finally hit their mark: *you are worth more.*

You are worth more than a sixty-hour workweek.

You are worth more than the rejection that split you in two.

You are worth more than the sum of your contributions to church and school and community.

You are worth more than a week of sleepless nights and crazy days trying to cross items off your to-do list.

You are worth more than your best outfit or good hair day.

You are worth more than your ability to make an unhappy friend happy.

You are worth more than the meanest person's criticism or the kindest person's praise.

So don't be afraid; you are worth more than many sparrows.

Jesus' words. Not mine. Did you notice the four-word command before His promise?

So don't be afraid.

In the previous verses, Jesus had been talking about our worry over provision—things like how we're going to pay the mortgage or buy food and clothes. But our panic over physical provision isn't all that different from our panic over heart provision. In both cases, we want to know we matter enough for a great big God to meet our greatest needs. So Jesus softly reminds us, as we scramble for a crust of bread or a scrap of attention, *you are worth more.*

Think of the various ways we measure and project value in our world. Cars, well-behaved children, houses, education, food, clothes, spirituality, philanthropy, contribution, intelligence. The list is long, isn't it? We've come up with a wealth of ways to measure value, and we use them to gauge the worth of ourselves and others. It's a wicked-fierce measuring stick, my friends, and we wonder why we don't feel all that great about ourselves and each other.

"So God created mankind in his own image," Genesis says (1:27). That means both you and me. Before we boasted wardrobes and degrees and hip hairstyles. Before we married, mothered, or collected an impressive list of community service projects. He made us. And He marveled at what He had done: "It was very good" (Gen. 1:31).

Time to put the radar into retirement. We don't need to gauge the praise and affection of every person we meet, nor do we need to make the unhappiest person in the room happy. Value isn't about appearance or effort or intellect or charm.

It's about the imprint you and I carry of the almighty God. I am His. You are His. And He's already confirmed "it is good."

Rest, dear ones. The most important person in the room already loves you.

Even the most successful careers and families cannot give the significance, security, and affirmation that the author of glory and love can.

—Timothy Keller, *The Reason for God*

Who Am I?

Time to get real. How do you measure human value? Annual income? Ability to carry on an intelligent conversation? Marital status or number of children? Church attendance? Like it or not, those of us who hold impossible standards for ourselves also wield those same unreachable standards against everyone else. I'm weary of the struggle, both the self-degradation and the judgments of others. How about you? When we believe our individual value in God's eyes, we're finally able to see something of the value of those around us.

Day 7

I Am

They will live in safety, and no one will make them afraid.

—EZEKIEL 34:28B

I give them eternal life and they shall never perish; no one will snatch them out of my hand.

—JOHN 10:28

By the time he was five years old, my dad had discovered that the world is not safe.

He was the youngest of three children, and his boyhood was traumatic. After his parents divorced, Dad found himself pulled between two dysfunctional homes. In one, alcoholism wreaked havoc. In the other, mental illness and promiscuity. I'll spare you the details, but trust me, it was nothing a child should ever know.

Somehow he stumbled through grade school and high school and made it to college before spending two years in the army and the Vietnam War. More pain, more trauma.

Until the day his life was spared when it shouldn't have been.

Somewhere outside of Phu Loi, Vietnam, the companies in front of and behind his were ambushed. His unit was spared. Months later he returned home to his young wife with a Bronze Star, physically unscathed. Less than a year later, I was born.

But Dad was never the same. He returned from war a different man, both for good and for bad. War, especially a politically charged one like Vietnam, has a way of tearing at the fabric of a man's soul. Even so, a small spark of new life had also taken hold. In spite of a lifetime of pain, he believed there had to be a reason he was still alive. So he started searching for its source, for the God his faith-filled grandma had often told him about.

A year later, a coworker invited him to church.

And that's when God started rebuilding the broken boy turned man. The world still wasn't safe, Dad knew that. He faced plenty more challenges, as we all do. But he'd found a refuge. A God who had laid down His life to save another's.

Some of you discovered that the world wasn't safe early in life, too. Perhaps you had a parent with mental illness. Or maybe a neighbor who took advantage of you. For some it was a teacher who constantly criticized or a foster care system that failed. The possibilities are so varied and painful, I can hardly write them out. Even beyond the acute traumas, ordinary days can be riddled with the unexpected.

Busy streets, sharp objects, threatening strangers. With each passing year, each step closer to adulthood, a child's fear is confirmed again and again. Danger is everywhere and hardship cannot be avoided.

This life can be dangerous and terrifying. Psalm 91 gives us a glimpse of the various sufferings we can expect:

- "the fowler's snare" (v. 3)
- "deadly pestilence" (v. 3)
- "the terror of night" (v. 5)
- "the arrow that flies by day" (v. 5)
- "the pestilence that stalks in the darkness" (v. 6)

- "the plague that destroys at midday" (v. 6)
- "a thousand may fall at your side" (v. 7)

That about covers it, don't you think? Disease. Conflict. Terrorism. Unrelenting fear. Injustice. Death. At morning, midday, and night. Under the cover of darkness or in the bright light of day. Pain will come. Period.

It sounds morbid and overwhelming. And it is. Unless we find the one place of safety even a war can't crush.

The psalmist knew this, which is why he doesn't leave us in a pit of despair. Instead, he describes a refuge so secure we can rest in spite of the war.

> *Whoever dwells in the shelter of the Most High*
> *will rest in the shadow of the Almighty.*
> *I will say of the* Lord, *"He is my refuge and my fortress,*
> *my God, in whom I trust."*
>
> —Psalm 91:1–2

Several chapters earlier, the writer in Psalm 31:2 said something similar: "Your granite cave a hiding place, your high cliff aerie a place of safety" (MSG).

There are seasons, however, when even this comfort doesn't make me feel better. Bad things happen, pain comes, loss steals life right out of my hand. And I wonder, Where is the safety of God in all this? The truth is I want a life free from pain. I want a marriage that doesn't ever struggle, children who always behave, a body that stays healthy, and relationships that are easy and uncomplicated. I don't want storms or wars or conflicts.

But I'm learning something, even as I fight against the fear.

Safety isn't the absence of suffering. It's finding rest in the middle of it.

"In this world you will have trouble. But take heart! I have overcome the world," Jesus said (John 16:33).

Choosing God as your safety doesn't mean the struggles will cease. The cave doesn't lessen the intensity of the storm outside. It doesn't still the thunder or cease the lightning or keep the rain from falling.

The cave provides a place of peace. Even when the storm continues to swirl.

This is what Dad discovered as he fought wars both at home and abroad. No, the world is not a safe place.

But there is no refuge like our God.

Away, then, all fears. The kingdom is safe in the King's hands.

—Charles Spurgeon, *Morning and Evening*

Who Am I?

What are you most afraid of? Financial insecurity? Illness? The future for a child who struggles? Loneliness in a hard marriage? Death? Whatever terrifies you, name it. Perhaps find an empty journal page and write it down. It's okay. God already knows. Now picture yourself in a cave, buffered from the elements, safe. This is God's cave, created for you. Even better, He is with you in it. Savor His presence, this God who sees you, knows you, and promises never to leave you. Tell Him your fears and ask Him to reassure you of His safety regardless of the storm.

Day 8

I Am

I will make a covenant of peace with them; it will be an everlasting covenant. I will establish them and increase their numbers, and I will put my sanctuary among them forever. My dwelling place will be with them, I will be their God, and they will be my people. Then the nations will know that I the Lord *make Israel holy, when my sanctuary is among them forever.*

—*Ezekiel 37:26–28*

My sharp response surprised even myself. One moment I was smiling. The next I was fuming.

What happened in the moments before wasn't necessarily earth shattering. The short of it is this: in front of a large group of people, someone I valued made a joke. At my expense. As a result, I felt humiliated in front of my peers, and not a little betrayed by someone I thought I could trust.

Twenty minutes later, out of earshot of the group, I pulled my friend aside and launched into a rebuttal. No benefit of the doubt. No patient dialogue or discussion of feelings. Instead, a full-on reaction to the wound I'd suffered.

Some might say I was justified. But I'm not so sure sharp words are ever justified. What horrified me most was how quickly anger bubbled to the surface and flew right out my mouth. "For the mouth speaks what the heart is full of," Jesus said (Luke 6:45). All it took was a friend's foolishness to bring out the ugly within.

That incident happened years ago. Unfortunately, I don't have to go so far back in time to see more evidence of my unholiness. If I count back a short seven days from today, I can unearth a mass of indicting evidence: I gossiped. I judged. I snapped and misspoke. I entertained vindictive thoughts. I resisted forgiving someone. I swore. I withheld love. Need I continue?

I'm far too familiar with myself to accept Ezekiel's proclamations of my holiness without protest. Holiness sits as far from my reach as going to sleep as a girl and waking up as a fish.

And yet God, through prophetic words, claims He not only holds the power to make me holy but also *has made it so*. Mind blowing.

Perhaps part of our struggle with personal holiness is that, over time, we've reduced being holy to following a set of rules. Merriam-Webster defines holy as "connected to a god or religion; religious and morally good." We've made holiness and morality interchangeable words, both meaning doing all the do's and avoiding all the don'ts.

In the process, we've cheapened the very meaning of holy. As a result, we fear it, shudder at the concept, knowing full well we have no power to obey a set of impossible rules.

The biblical definition of holiness is quite different from Merriam-Webster's. According to the Bible, to be holy is to be set apart or dedicated to God. To belong to Him, first and foremost. Although morality is certainly part of the equation, it's more a response to God's work than a precursor to it. Holiness is first and foremost about relationship.

"I the Lord make Israel holy, when my sanctuary is among them forever."

When my sanctuary is among them forever.

I grew up thinking the sanctuary was that long, steepled room lined with hard wooden pews. I sat there every Sunday morning, eyes front and center on the pulpit and choir loft. That's a sanctuary, right?

Not exactly. In the Old Testament, the Israelites carried around with them a portable tent—a tabernacle—which was the place where God dwelled. It was a literal place, a sanctuary or "house" for God.

Then Jesus came. The actual dwelling of God in human flesh. He became the tabernacle for us, the human house for the presence of God with man. Thus Isaiah called Him "Immanuel, God with us" (7:14).

Wait. It gets better.

When Jesus told the disciples He needed to leave to return to the Father, their response was panic. If Jesus left, that meant God was leaving. They'd waited their whole lives for God to come to them in the form of the Messiah.

And now He planned to take off?

Jesus explained: "But very truly I tell you, it is for your good that I am going away. Unless I go away, the Advocate will not come to you; but if I go, I will send him to you" (John 16:7).

This promised Spirit—the one Jesus said would come when He left—is the presence of the Holy Spirit in us.

Go ahead. Read that again.

The presence of the living God *in us*.

The tabernacle is no longer a portable tent in the desert. It's not even the human flesh-and-blood body of Jesus. The sanctuary is *us*. We carry around the living presence of a holy God in the form of His Spirit, until the day you and I stand in the throne room of heaven and see our God face to face.

Glory!

The Holy Spirit. In us.

Which, my friends, makes us holy.

Not because we earned it. Not because we followed a set of moral rules.

But because of the mercy of God, who made it so.

Chances are I'll collect plenty more evidence of my unholiness before tomorrow. Another impatient response or selfish decision. No matter how hard I try, I can't escape my humanity.

But as a follower of Jesus, I can't escape His holiness either. He lives in me, in both my moments of shame and my moments of success, changing me, helping me to grow. He won't subject me to public ridicule. Instead, He'll fill me with Himself, making me holy one day at a time with Himself.

If we would ripen in grace, we must live near to Jesus—in His presence—ripened by the sunshine of His smiles. We must hold sweet communion with Him. We must leave the distant view of His face and come near, as John did, and pillow our head on His breast; then shall we find ourselves advancing in holiness.

—Charles Spurgeon, *Morning and Evening*

Who Am I?

I can hardly fathom the fact that you and I have been made holy. God's very presence lives in you. In me. How does that make you feel? Terrified? Relieved? Overwhelmed? Comforted? Maybe all of the above. Now for the tough question: How does the truth of God's presence *in you* impact how you desire to think, speak, feel, and behave today? Be courageous. Be specific. Then ask the Spirit to, by His power, make it so.

Day 9

I Am Treasured

Since you are precious and honored in my sight, and because I love you.

—Isaiah 43:4

It sits in the top corner of my closet, covered in dust. But don't let the dust fool you. Treasure hides inside.

Old books bury it, as well as random papers and a giant plastic tub of last winter's clothes. An outsider would never notice it amid all the clutter. Smaller than a shoebox, it was made of wood by unknown hands decades ago. The box itself is nothing special. Without lining, engraving, or decor of any kind. It is stained a deep, rich mahogany with tarnished brass braces that hug the lid to the base. Marred long before my time, littered with scratches on its cover and sides.

Inside, I've collected my most treasured items. Nothing of real monetary value, nothing the world would chase after, but items that mean the world to me just the same. These are the things I'd grab in a fire.

The bedtime book I read to my children so many times over the years that I've memorized each word.

My grandfather's royal blue handkerchief, embroidered with small white flowers.

A collection of silver dollars given to me by my grandmother, a woman I didn't have enough time to know.

A short, handwritten love note on a torn scrap of paper from my soft-spoken husband.

Behind each treasure sits a story. And behind each story stands a person. And behind each person lies a deep well of love.

It takes a lot for something to become treasure-box worthy. Not every trinket ends up with sacred space. Plenty of vacation memorabilia and homemade cards never make it to the twelve-by-eight-inch mahogany womb. They may end up in a tub in the crawl space or stacked high on that same shelf in my bedroom closet. Valuable? Yes, of course. But the items inside the treasure box are more than valuable.

They're irreplaceable.

I've long dreamed of being that kind of priceless, of being treasure-box worthy.

As a young girl, I believed I'd find my treasure status in a relationship with a man. So I got married. But marriage didn't resolve my insatiable need for significance.

Then I turned to mothering. Surely motherhood would give me a constant assurance of significance.

Pardon me while I spew coffee out my nose.

I enjoy being a parent and love my children more than words can say. But my attempts to earn my worth through mothering usually evaporate by midafternoon, when the complaints and needs and never-ending crises zap the last of my patience.

So I focused on my work. If I couldn't be treasure-box worthy in marriage and mothering, I could take a serious shot at it with my career. Then followed long hours and impossible expectations. The moment one project was completed, another three took its place. The work was never done. Worse? I was exhausted from trying.

Day 9

It's what we all do to some extent, isn't it? Behind our tireless striving lies a deep desire to prove our worth, to display our merit and achieve treasure-box status.

Yet it doesn't take long to discover we're fatally flawed. In spite of our best efforts, we look far more like the beat-up box than a treasure worthy of hiding inside. Value? What value? Then, consumed as we are with our insignificance, we turn around and use the same impossible scale to weigh everyone else.

Thank heaven, God chooses His treasures a different way.

But now, this is what the Lord says—
he who created you, Jacob,
he who formed you, Israel:
"Do not fear, for I have redeemed you;
I have summoned you by name; you are mine.
When you pass through the waters,
I will be with you;
and when you pass through the rivers,
they will not sweep over you.
When you walk through the fire,
you will not be burned;
the flames will not set you ablaze.
For I am the Lord your God,
the Holy One of Israel, your Savior;
I give Egypt for your ransom,
Cush and Seba in your stead.
Since you are precious and honored in my sight,
and because I love you."

—Isaiah 43:1–4

God has an eye for treasure. When He looks at us, He doesn't see a worn and worthless trinket. He sees a story. And a person behind the story. And a love beyond comprehension.

All those days and years spent trying to earn treasure-box status? Unnecessary. All that worry over whether you'll measure up? A waste. You've already been deemed precious and honored.

Exhale, my friend. You're worth grabbing in a fire. No more killing yourself trying to secure sacred space in the divine's box of incomparable treasure.

You already have it.

In a world that relentlessly reduces us to skin and bones, our God speaks abundant, outrageous life. He creates. He renovates. He turns trash into treasure, fish into a feast, and a nearly invisible grain of faith into a mountain-moving force.

—Bo Stern, *Ruthless*

Who Am I?

My heart finds great relief in the fact that God doesn't use human scales to weigh my worth. His approach is quite the opposite. But although I'm relieved, I also feel convicted. When it comes to treasuring people, too often I resort to critical standards. I measure worth based on appearance and performance, even while I hope others don't do the same to me. Today consider how well you treasure human life, both yourself and others. Then ask God to give you eyes to see the people and possessions and purposes of this life as He does.

Day 10

I Am Known

I know my sheep and my sheep know me.

—John 10:14

We met for coffee as we'd done many times before. After spending months confined to my house, too sick to leave, it felt good to do something ordinary. Even so, I entered the coffee shop wrapped in a blanket of sadness I couldn't seem to shake. While I appreciated the health that allowed me a date, the memory of what I had endured in the months before was far stronger than the coffee shop's dark roast.

Latte in hand, I sat down and tried to keep my emotions tucked safely away.

"Hey there!" My attempt at a smile was poor at best. She didn't seem to notice.

"It's so good to see you!" Her joy seemed far more sincere. I envied her that.

For the next several minutes, we settled into small talk about the day, our families, the week's activities. It was nice, sharing normal conversation. But my sadness wouldn't leave me alone. So when she asked me how I was doing, I decided to tell the truth.

"I'm sad. A lot. Can't seem to stop crying."

"Sad?" She pulled her brows together in a giant question mark. "Why?"

With that one-word question, I knew: she didn't understand. She didn't have a clue what cancer had cost me.

The truth of this stung. My friend didn't intend to hurt me. She just couldn't fathom the reason for my sadness. So in the space of two seconds, my sadness grew complicated by another emotion: aloneness.

This same scene repeated itself multiple times in the months that followed with various friends and family. After nearly succumbing to this third cancer occurrence, friends and family celebrated the gift of my life. They looked at me, altered as I was, and saw someone who shouldn't have survived the hell she endured. A miracle! A gift! They didn't see what had been lost, only what had been gained—life. And so they danced and celebrated and expected me to do the same.

Only I couldn't. Instead, I mourned. I mourned the innocence of believing I'd live a long life. I mourned the loss of a body that worked as it should, looked as it should. And because those closest to me couldn't grasp my grief, I mourned the aloneness that resulted.

I wanted to be known, understood. But it seemed no one could bridge the gap of experience to offer it.

There are few things as painful as being misunderstood.

A friend misinterprets your email. A coworker questions your integrity. A spouse doubts your fidelity. Regardless of the circumstance, to be misunderstood is to discover, to your great sadness, that the one who should know you best doesn't really know you at all.

True empathy is a nearly impossible endeavor. It's neither easy nor comfortable to step into another's experience. Part of this is because of our natural human limitations; we don't understand the roads we haven't walked. But to be blunt, sometimes we don't understand simply because we don't want to. We don't want to ask questions. We don't want to sacrifice the time it takes to listen. And we don't want to share another's pain and pay the price of knowing.

Perhaps this is why I found myself drawing closer to the cross. For most of my life, I've celebrated Jesus' resurrection. He is alive! I certainly need the gift of His life, and so I danced around His empty tomb with great celebration.

But in this season of suffering, I also needed Jesus' grief and death. I needed to know a God who suffered, because I suffered. I needed to know a God who felt pain, because then He knew something of my pain.

In the Golgotha of my agony, I finally understand the comfort of the cross. At the broken body of Jesus, I finally feel known and understood. It is there, where both Jesus and I weep for all that's been lost, that I am safe enough to say, "I'm not okay." I'm no longer shamed into silence or looked at with confusion. Instead, Jesus' eyes meet mine, and somehow I know that *He knows*.

God does not expect me to dance at His empty tomb without weeping at His cross. I don't have to hide my grief or pretend I'm stronger than I am. Instead, I am blessed to have a Savior who steps into my story, who understands me more than any mother, father, husband, or friend ever can.

"I have summoned you by name, you are mine," God says (Isa. 43:1). This is why He came. This is why He left the light of heaven for the pain of a cross.

So He could meet us there. And I'd finally know I'm known.

To be loved but not known is comforting but superficial. To be known and not loved is our greatest fear. But to be fully known and truly loved is, well, a lot like being loved by God. It is what we need more than anything. It liberates us from pretense, humbles us out of our self-righteousness, and fortifies us for any difficulty life can throw at us.

—Timothy Keller, *The Meaning of Marriage*

Who Am I?

You and I don't always grasp the significance of the cross. It's hard to watch, painful to take in. And yet we find as much comfort at the cross as we do at the empty tomb. It is Jesus' suffering that gives celebration to His resurrection. Today, sit at the cross. Don't try to fill the silence with words. Instead, see your Savior suffering, choosing death so you could have life. Choosing to be misunderstood so you would be known.

Part 2

Exodus

Day 11

I Am Sinful

Rid yourselves of all the offenses you have committed, and get a new heart and a new spirit. Why will you die, people of Israel? For I take no pleasure in the death of anyone, declares the Sovereign Lord. Repent and live!

—Ezekiel 18:31–32

Sin is a hard word for me to take.

I don't like to think of myself as sinful. I'm a good person. It's already noon and I haven't robbed a bank or committed any violent crimes. I made breakfast for my family, tackled a sink full of dishes, and read my Bible.

I even prayed. How about some bonus points for this girl?

Sinful? No, thank you. Not good for my self-esteem. I'd prefer to come up with something less offensive. Imperfect, maybe? A woman with a few rough edges, perhaps? How about "in progress"? That's much more my style.

I desperately want to believe I'm good at heart, that I'm above the temptation to inflict pain on another. I'm kind and generous, patient and thoughtful.

For the most part.

As a whole, we don't enjoy the word sin. Let's just say it doesn't make for good party conversation. The sound scrapes the soul like fingernails on a chalkboard, making us cringe.

Yet most of us wouldn't deny sin's existence or influence. Click on your news app and you'll see enough evidence of sin in the first five minutes to make you want to hurl.

The stranger who kidnapped and murdered a grade-school girl.

The two parents who severely neglected their three children.

The college coach who grossly abused his position.

The CEO who scammed thousands of their retirement funds.

The pastor who grew too proud of his own press.

Evil shows up in the craziest places, yes? We can't avoid it. And yet avoid it I do. Especially when it comes to myself. Let's put it this way. If I were to grade myself on behavior, I'd probably award myself a solid B. Maybe not an A, because of that incident with the man-child last week when he exploded his spaghetti and marinara in the microwave and didn't clean it up. I might've exploded a bit myself. I'm only human, right?

Right. That's the point.

I often don't have to look any farther than my own home to find the sin lurking within. It explains how quickly I transition from calm to chaos if someone hurls an accusation my direction. And what about the fact that my patience and quantity of sleep seem to be directly related to each other? And I haven't even begun to expose the chronic insecurity that can make me either passive-aggressive or outright heinous. As if it's all about me anyway.

Sin, by definition, is anything that sets itself up against the holiness and glory of God. Sin isn't measured in grades, with A's, B's, and C's being given to those who do a fair job of keeping it at bay and D's and F's to those who succumb to its worst forms. Sin is a pass-fail scenario. Either you have it or you don't.

When my husband and I recently applied for a home mortgage, the loan officer filling out our application asked, "Do you have any debt?"

If you're debt conscious and work to avoid it, you'd likely answer that question with a hint of pride:

- "We're debt free except for our mortgage."
- "We don't have any debt aside from one credit card."
- "One car payment. That's it. Otherwise, we're debt free."

But that wasn't the loan officer's question. His question wasn't one of degree. It was pass-fail.

Do you have any debt?

Only two options: yes or no.

And whether my debt is a lie, a cheat, or an explosion over a marinara-christened microwave, my answer can only be yes. A thousand times yes.

For a long time I feared that the admission of my sin would be painful. And it was. Until I understood grace, of the God variety. God's grace isn't a flimsy excusing of my poor behavior. It isn't a casual, "I'm only human after all." It's a gift of cash in full acknowledgment of the impossible debt.

For too long I fooled myself into believing that I carried less debt than the next guy. All that did was make me more desperate to earn a better grade. I thought my salvation depended on what I brought to the loan officer's table. But when I admitted it, fully and freely, I found nothing but sweet relief.

"Whoever conceals their sins does not prosper, but the one who confesses and renounces them finds mercy" (Prov. 28:13).

Do you have any debt? Yes, you do. Loads of it. So do I.

We're sinful, through and through. Go ahead and say it out loud, without fear. Sadness, yes. Regret, no doubt. But you needn't fear the admission.

Because when you and I chose Jesus, He paid it all. The debt is gone.

"I'm only human" is no longer an excuse for your bad behavior or mine. It's merely evidence of our desperate need for a Savior. No more, no less.

Isn't it time we dare to get real about sin? I know it's hard, but ignoring the truth is costly. But owning it—our sin and sinfulness—moves us a giant step toward making peace with who we are. Only the sinful need a Savior. My identity is no longer "sinner." My identity is "saved."

My sin, oh, the bliss of this glorious thought!
My sin, not in part but the whole,
Is nailed to the cross, and I bear it no more,
Praise the Lord, praise the Lord, O my soul!

—Horatio G. Spafford, "It Is Well with My Soul"

Who Am I?

In our culture, sin is an antiquated word that is often avoided. Instead, we choose less-confrontational words to take its place, words like mistake or misstep. But these words not only minimize our actions and their effects but minimize our need for a Savior. In our attempts to soften our sense of responsibility, we've also weakened our sense of wonder at the rescue, the fact that someone greater than us has gone to great lengths to make right our wrongs. It's the admission of sinfulness that frees us to embrace the solution: the undeserved mercy of a loving God. Today, dare to face your sinfulness. Not as a means to shame but as a first step toward salvation.

Day 12

My people have been lost sheep; their shepherds have led them astray and caused them to roam on the mountains. They wandered over mountain and hill and forgot their own resting place.

—Jeremiah 50:6

For the Son of Man came to seek and to save the lost.

—Luke 19:10

The clock on the dash of my Toyota 4-Runner flashed 11:38 p.m.

Well past my 9:00 p.m. bedtime. Ahem.

With each mile I drove in the dark, my only thought was of sleep. The warmth of my cozy pajamas. The comfort of sliding beneath a hefty cocoon of blankets and comforters and succumbing to the slumber I'd been holding at bay for two and a half hours. Exhausted didn't even begin to describe it.

One look out my windshield, however, confirmed I was lost.

Driving through the Rocky Mountains is beautiful in the daytime. Thick forests, towering peaks, curving roads, and surprise glimpses of wildlife. Breathtaking in every way.

Driving through those same mountains at night, however, is another thing altogether. It's like navigating a maze blindfolded. What hours before had seemed welcoming had now become frightening, as if nature itself might swallow me up and no one would ever know.

No street lights illuminated the road. Clouds dimmed the moon and stars, leaving just my car headlights to find the way. A cabin and writing retreat waited on the other side of this adventure, I reassured myself. But only if I found my way there. I searched for signs and landmarks, but nothing appeared familiar in the dark.

It's a tough thing to admit you're lost, especially when you think you should know where to go. I had directions to the mountain cabin, had even been there before. But a change in scenery and a lack of both sleep and light made it difficult to find my way.

In all, my lostness lasted no more than a half hour. A long half hour, mind you, but by the time I crawled into bed, I'd already forgotten the fear of losing my way.

I've stumbled through seasons of darkness that plagued me far longer than thirty minutes. And the terror of those months and years isn't something I'll soon forget.

It's one thing to be lost on a mountain road. It's another thing to be lost in your own life. To end up someplace you never dreamed, taking in scenery you don't recognize, wishing you were anywhere but here. To wake up one day and discover you have no idea where you are, where you're going, or even how to get back to the life you once had.

You've probably experienced moments like this.

When a move to another state or city drops you in the middle of a neighborhood and community with which you're completely unfamiliar.

When you first drive home from the hospital with eight pounds of bundled little person buckled in the back seat and you realize—gasp!—that those parenting books you read didn't really prepare you for the adventure of parenting.

When a church endures a crisis or, heaven forbid, a brutal split, leaving you without a safe, spiritual family.

When your kids grow up and move out, forcing you into a season of empty nesting that feels as foreign as parenting did once upon a time.

The examples are endless, but the feeling is much the same. Lost in unfamiliar territory. Anxious. Desperate to find your way through the wilderness to a place that feels like home.

It has taken me decades, but I'm finally starting to understand. For too long, when circumstances left me feeling lost, I rolled up my sleeves to take control. To work hard and move to a place of my choosing, one that felt more comfortable, more predictable, more safe. But as soon as I approached a new destination, it too disappeared over the horizon. Always out of reach, always beyond my grasp.

But now I know. Home isn't a place I pursue or a destination I achieve.

Home is Jesus.

And resting in who He is, right here.

Even in this new neighborhood and unfamiliar community, Jesus is my home and I take Him wherever I go.

Even through parenting's many land mines, God is the single best resource for how to parent my children. He'll give me exactly the wisdom I need when I need it.

Even when churches fail and fall apart, God can heal a riff-raff collection of lost people and show them how better to live.

Home is allowing Him to lead me into new and unexpected territory, trusting that although I may find it unfamiliar, He has already gone before. He knows the way, and He won't leave me lost and alone.

It's not easy to admit our lostness. It's tempting to put both hands on the wheel and determine our own way. But the danger of that is our knack for remaining lost.

If you're lost in a place you never imagined you'd end up, admit you need some help to get back home. It's the first step, like slowing down to ask for directions. We have access to a God who knows how to get us headed the right direction. We don't need a map or GPS. We don't have to scour the road for signs and landmarks.

Our God is here, now.

That means we're already home.

Amazing grace, how sweet the sound,
That saved a wretch like me!
I once was lost but now I'm found,
Was blind but now I see.

—John Newton, "Amazing Grace"

Who Am I?

Many jokes have been made at the expense of men who won't stop to ask for directions. Why? Because we all know a simple admission would solve the problem. But are you and I any different? Think about your current life location. Like assigning GPS coordinates to your real-time scenario, be specific. Are you where you planned to be? What situations make you feel a bit lost? And when's the last time you stopped long enough to ask for God's direction? It's never too late. Admit your lostness and let Him show you the way home.

Day 13

I Am Fought For

I will make you a wall to this people, a fortified wall of bronze; they will fight against you but will not overcome you, for I am with you to rescue and save you.

—Jeremiah 15:20

He came home one day from seventh grade on the verge of tears.

Of course, he tried to deny it, to blink away the evidence. But I knew better. This was my tenderhearted boy. The one whose well of emotion ran deep, the one who could never hide either his joy or his pain.

It took mere minutes of maternal questioning before he finally caved: bullies.

Two of them. Fellow seventh graders. These were kids he'd once called friends in early grade school. Now they were making an ordinary school day a nightmare. It had been going on for a few weeks, he said. In Spanish class they openly mocked him, hurling insults in front of the entire class, including a passive teacher. At the end of each day, as he rushed to grab his backpack and catch the bus home, they blocked his way or pushed him to the ground.

Mean. Nothing but middle school meanness.

In seconds, I morphed from gentle mama comforting her baby to raging bear on the verge of attack. *No one hurts my child!* I grabbed my phone, ready to punch in the ten numbers for the school office and expose the bullies to the staff.

Then, a better idea. A face-to-face beat down! I grabbed my car keys, ready to give those boys a talking-to they'd never forget.

"Please, Mom. Don't."

My boy's plea stopped me in my tracks.

"I don't want you to do anything, Mom. I'll take care of it. Please."

Now, I know there are times when bullying needs to be confronted and stopped. I've read enough heartwrenching news stories to know the seriousness of adolescent taunts. But in this case, I could also see my son's perspective. He wanted a chance to stand up to them, to handle it himself without running away. Reluctantly—and after much deep breathing—I agreed.

Within a short time, my son had handled the situation and the bullies had backed off. And he'd found a solid group of close friends—his cross-country teammates—who provided a safe circle of friendship throughout his high school years.

Even better, he found himself. He came to see his own value, something no bully could take away. That confidence serves him well to this day.

I've thought hard and often about those precarious weeks in seventh grade. It could've turned out differently. I still have moments when I question my decision to back off. And yet perhaps what my boy needed most I'd already provided: a promise to go to battle for him.

He needed to know he had someone in his corner. The fact that I was furious with those seventh-grade boys helped him to recognize the injustice of it. It also gave him courage to stand up to them.

I may not have driven to the school or picked up the phone, but I fought for him just the same. I fought for his sense of value. I fought for his dwindling courage. And I fought for him to discover that no one, no matter how seemingly powerful, can steal who we are. Ever.

To a seventh-grade boy trying to find his way, those truths proved the difference between success and failure on the middle school battlefield.

Our battles may no longer include twelve-year-old bullies, but every one of us—child and adult alike—need to know there is someone in our corner. When we're up against a fight, something that feels far beyond our ability to win, our strength is revived when we know we're not alone.

This is clearly seen in Exodus 14, when Moses and the Israelites find themselves backed up against the Red Sea. With an army of angry Egyptians pursuing from behind, they must press forward or be overcome. But how does a beat-down group of former slaves swim across an ocean?

In that moment, faced with personal frailty and the Egyptians' cruelty, the Israelites panicked. They'd endured much, waiting for their freedom. Now it seemed they had no way out. Fear and doubt pressed in as hard as the approaching Egyptian army.

That's when God spoke up through Moses: "Do not be afraid. Stand firm and you will see the deliverance the LORD will bring you today. The Egyptians you see today you will never see again. The LORD will fight for you; you need only to be still" (Ex. 14:13–14).

I can almost hear God's fiery pronouncement: *no one hurts my children!*

In the moments that followed, God did indeed fight for His children. He didn't swoop down with sword and chariot to cut down the Egyptians. Instead, in dramatic display, He parted the Red Sea, allowing His children to pass through. Once they arrived safely on the other side, He allowed the waters to return to their place, swallowing up the Egyptian pursuers.

This isn't the only biblical evidence of God's willingness to go to battle for those He loves. He did the same when:

- King Jehoshaphat faced a "vast army" (2 Chron. 20:15).
- Joshua and the Israelites fought for Jericho (Joshua 5 and 6).
- Joseph, Mary, and an infant Jesus fled a jealous king (Matt. 2:13–18).

- A world filled with broken, desperate people prayed for a Savior (John 3:16–17).

We have a God who fights for us. At times I want His fight to look like the elimination of all pain and suffering. I want Him to swing His sword at every injustice, every disease, every evil. At times, that's what He does.

But like a mama who stayed close to her boy, helping him find the faith to navigate the world of middle school bullies, sometimes our God fights for us in ways we didn't imagine. He doesn't remove the battle, but He walks with us through it.

Either way, our God never leaves us alone on the battlefield.

He fights for His children. To the very end. And He always wins.

When I let God fight for me, He always wins.

—Bo Stern, *Ruthless*

Who Am I?

It can be difficult to understand the ways God fights for us, especially when we pray and circumstances don't seem to change. Honestly, some days God seems more passive than active, especially when I'm most desperate for deliverance. Psalm 121:4 says God will "neither slumber nor sleep." When it comes to your life and mine, He's always on duty. How might He be working in your life even now? Think back on His faithfulness in the past, and ask Him to show you His activity in the present.

Day 14

I Am Proud

"Let not the wise boast of their wisdom or the strong boast of their strength or the rich boast of their riches, but let the one who boasts boast about this: that they have the understanding to know me, that I am the Lord, who exercises kindness, justice and righteousness on earth, for in these I delight," declares the Lord.

—Jeremiah 9:23–24

We call her Peanut. A term of endearment and evidence of her small stature. She's a tiny slip of a girl, much smaller than the other eight-year-olds she calls her friends.

Don't let her size fool you, however. She's also a pistol. Full of spit and fire and blessed with an unyielding will. She bosses anything that breathes and assumes control of whatever room she enters.

Including mine. At least, she gives it a solid try.

"Peanut, I need you to go pick up your room, please."

"No," she shrugs, continuing to play, unmoved by my request.

"You also need to finish your homework before you go outside."

"I don't want to," she announces with a lift of her chin as she walks out the front door.

I haul her stubborn self back inside, along with her stomping feet. She's met her match in me. I'm equally independent, with an added three decades of practice. Let's just say I've honed the craft. And I'm not going to let a forty-pound peanut hijack my well-ordered house. No matter her spit and fire.

One of the greatest gifts my dad gave me was a sense of independence. He never made me feel less than strong or able because of my femaleness. Dad forced me to stand on my own and take responsibility for my life. At times, these were hard lessons for a small girl to learn. As a woman, however, I understood their value. These skills serve me well to this day.

But independence also fostered something less attractive: stubborn pride. A determination to do things alone, without needing any outside help. To work hard and take control. To keep all details and decisions squarely in the palms of my own two hands.

This may benefit me up to a point, but unchecked pride eventually fosters nothing but isolation.

This is true for both human and spiritual relationships. From the beginning, we were wired for community. First and foremost with our Creator, second with each other. Even in the perfection of the garden, Adam and Eve required food for sustenance of the body and the presence of God for sustenance of the soul. From the moment of conception, we were marked as the created, not the Creator. We're fully dependent on God for survival.

And yet how often we forget!

We are proud. Independent. Determined to control our days and destinies.

Only we can't. And sooner or later this truth becomes harsh reality. Often it takes a tragedy or hardship we couldn't predict or prevent to finally recognize the foolishness of our pride. When the doctor calls with bad news despite all the exercise we did and the organic food we ate. When our child gets kicked out of school despite our stellar parenting and our lectures about choices and consequences. When, despite our excellent money management, the housing market collapses.

What value is our pride and independence then?

Pride has plagued people from the beginning. Pride tempted Eve to eat the forbidden fruit. Pride led Adam, her husband, to follow suit and then blame her for doing so. It was pride that caused Cain to murder his brother Abel, pride that led David to murder his lover's husband, pride that led even the wise Solomon to take for himself countless wives and mistresses. It causes us to ignore the twinge of conscience when we tread a dangerous line or refuse the lifegiving rebuke of a friend. Pride says, "No, I don't want to," or, "Leave me be, I can do this myself!"

Pride refuses counsel, denies leadership, ignores sovereignty. It demands its own way, regardless of the cost. And pride always costs far more than we imagine.

- "The Lord detests all the proud of heart. Be sure of this: They will not go unpunished" (Prov. 16:5).
- "Pride goes before destruction, a haughty spirit before a fall" (Prov. 16:18).
- "Cursed is the one who trusts in man, who draws strength from mere flesh and whose heart turns away from the Lord" (Jer. 17:5).

And yet humility—that awareness of our need and admission of dependency—comes with incredible reward:

- "When pride comes, then comes disgrace, but with humility comes wisdom" (Prov. 11:2).
- "Whoever disregards discipline comes to poverty and shame, but whoever heeds correction is honored" (Prov. 13:18).

Pride is a tough topic to face, and releasing it makes us feel like we might lose something of ourselves in the process. But the opposite is true. Humility sets us free, placing us at the mercy of a Father who loves us far more than we can imagine. We no longer have to have all the answers or walk through this life on our own.

The next time we're tempted to lift our chin and march out the front door to take control of this one short life, let's reconsider. We have a God whose wisdom has no limits and whose love knows no end. He has promised to lead us into a life we can't imagine. We can do it our way, with our peanut-sized perspective, or we can do it His, with His eternal one.

Let's choose the latter. The love and leadership of God can be trusted. Always.

If you have wealth, do not glory in it, nor in friends because they are powerful, but in God Who gives all things and Who desires above all to give Himself. Do not boast of personal stature or of physical beauty, qualities which are marred and destroyed by a little sickness. Do not take pride in your talent or ability, lest you displease God to Whom belongs all the natural gifts that you have.

—Thomas á Kempis, *The Imitation of Christ*

Who Am I?

On a scale of 1 to 10, how self-sufficient are you in your spiritual life? Often, relinquishing control to the sovereign God is easy in some areas, far more difficult in others. For example, it may be easy to trust God with your finances, but difficult to allow His leadership in your marriage. Consider any areas of your life where pride may be interfering with your freedom. Releasing control can feel scary at first, but ultimately it delivers relief and freedom. Take a few moments to admit your fears. Ask God to heal your insecurity and reassure you of His faithfulness and all sufficiency. He will give you the courage you need to trust Him.

Day 15

I Am *Not Abandoned*

Have I not commanded you? Be strong and courageous. Do not be afraid; do not be discouraged, for the Lord *your God will be with you wherever you go.*

—*Joshua 1:9*

I woke up early that Friday morning without the faintest clue of what the day would hold.

July 20, 2012.

I flipped on the news, as I often do. Then, scenes of Aurora, Colorado's Century 16 movie theater. Dozens of police cars and news crews, and word of dozens of people injured by the gunfire of a deranged killer. Many still unaccounted for.

Just that fast, horrific reality settled into a previously ordinary Friday like cement in my stomach.

Why? Oh, God, why?

Even then, even as I watched the news like a spectator, I didn't know that later that day I'd end up at Gateway High School, the gathering place for family members awaiting word of survivors. I didn't know I'd sit with a friend for eight hours as she waited for news of her son. Didn't know that later that night we'd receive confirmation of his death, even as nine other families learned of the deaths of their loved ones. Didn't know that over the course of a weekend, I would witness a depth of grief that made my own bones ache in agony.

I did not lose a son or a spouse that day. But I lost a hefty chunk of my innocence. Twelve people gone in a moment, in a horrific way. For four days, I walked through the nightmare with my friend. I experienced the agonizing wait while families counted the minutes until they received feared news of a son, daughter, boyfriend, girlfriend, mom, dad. I watched shoulders shake and bodies crumble under the weight of devastation. I heard groans carrying enough lament to split the sky. Even as I write, I know I will never forget the wails or faces of those who grieved.

As vivid as those images and sounds were, a scene shining like a light in the dark is what I saw when I first stepped inside Gateway High School that Friday afternoon: twelve round tables circled by the weeping. And centered on each table like a bastion, a copy of the New King James Holy Bible.

I noticed the Bibles right away, at first surprised that "God" had somehow been allowed admittance. Then I felt calmed, knowing God Himself had infiltrated the terror and torment of that room with His presence long before I did. I reached for one of the thick black-covered books, caressed the cover and pulled it close. I needed God's presence more than air.

I still do. The older I get, the more terrifying this life can be. In the past fifteen years, we've endured the Indian Ocean tsunami, the Sandy Hook school shooting, the Boston Marathon bombing, the Nepal earthquake, the Paris terrorist attacks. To name a few. Not to mention hurricanes. Recessions. Human trafficking. Homicides. Accidents. Disease. Wildfires. Suicides.

These dramas are not a collection of two-hour action-packed movies from which I can exit the theater and reenter a happier life.

This is real. Drama in shocking proximity. The truth of this should shake us all by the shoulders.

What if the worst happens?

It's a fair question, a real possibility.

When a large-scale tragedy, or threat of it, shakes the world, people often respond one of two ways: they turn away from God or toward Him. The first believes the tragedy strikes as a result of God's absence or abandonment. How could a good God allow this to happen? The second believes God is the only refuge and answer for a world gone awry.

"And surely I am with you always, to the very end of the age," Jesus said (Matt. 28:20). Words of comfort and strength to a world filled with people who needed to know they wouldn't be left on their own.

He's unruffled by the news, even if we aren't. Because He holds all things in His hands, including us. No matter how violently the earth shakes, He remains steadfast. That means we are not abandoned. No matter how bad it gets.

I have no answers for why bad things happen, no platitudes or easy retorts.

But this I know: whether or not we acknowledge Him, God is with us. His nearness is as tangible and sure as twelve black Bibles on twelve round tables. Our doubts and questions don't diminish His reality. He is the bedrock below our ever-shifting circumstantial sand. Someone who sees all, knows all, and promises it will be okay. Even better, someone who will be with us even when the worst happens.

There will be a reckoning, a day when a real God carries through on His promise: "He will wipe every tear from their eyes. There will be no more death or mourning or crying or pain." Rather than say it with a whisper, He will command it with a shout: "No more! *No more!*"

With the lament of a grieving Father, He will right all wrongs. How bleeding hearts long for that day! Until then, we wait. We cry. We live and lose, wail and pray. And we circle our chairs, alternately grieving and comforting each other, with this truth our unwavering bastion: rest assured, we are not abandoned. God will never walk away. He is *with* us, to the end of time.

Day 15

As a child may cry out in pain even when sheltered in its mother's arms, so a Christian may sometimes know what it is to suffer even in the conscious presence of God . . . But all will be well. In a world like this tears have their therapeutic effects. The healing balm distilled from the garments of the enfolding Presence cures our ills before they become fatal. The knowledge that we are never alone calms the troubled sea of our lives and speaks peace to our souls.

—A. W. Tozer, *The Knowledge of the Holy*

Who Am I?

To be abandoned brings the double sting of aloneness and rejection. It's not only isolation but isolation as a result of someone's choosing to walk away. If you've ever been abandoned—by a parent or spouse or friend—you know the deep wound left behind. You may not understand why God behaves as He does, why He seemingly allows people to suffer and children to die and evil to thrive. And yet His presence is certain in spite of all the pain. He will not abandon us! *We need You, God. More than ever. Help us to see You.*

Day 16

I Am Hungry

Come, all you who are thirsty, come to the waters; and you who have no money, come, buy and eat! Come, buy wine and milk without money and without cost. Why spend money on what is not bread, and your labor on what does not satisfy? Listen, listen to me, and eat what is good, and you will delight in the richest of fare. Give ear and come to me, listen, that you may live.

—Isaiah 55:1–3

At nine pounds, five ounces, my son Jacob came into this world expecting an all-you-can-eat buffet.

From the first cry, he made it clear he was hungry. Starving, in fact. In a nursery filled with sleeping six- and seven-pound baby boys and girls, my chunky monkey looked like a toddler. Or an exploding can of biscuits. Every time I hobbled to the window and asked to see him, the nurses grinned and cast me a nod in deference to my Herculean efforts to deliver the hungry man-child.

When we left the hospital two days later, the nurses didn't bother to send home any newborn diapers. Jacob had already outgrown them.

Instead, they gave us some size one pants and encouraged us to go shopping. Soon and often. All those precious newborn booties and blankets and outfits? Returned and exchanged faster than you could say, "Supersize me!" And every single blessed morning, at the first sound of his stirring, I flew out of bed to feed him before the screaming commenced.

"Give that kid a steak!" someone once remarked.

I considered it.

It's been nearly nineteen years since my man-baby entered the world. To this day, my six-foot, two-inch son still spends his every waking moment thinking of food. This week he informed me his goal is to ingest between 6,000 and 8,000 calories a day. A. Day.

Heaven help me, we're now accepting donations.

Breakfast consists of four or five scrambled eggs, toast, yogurt, sausages, and fruit. Four hot dogs—with buns—plus whatever potato chips and various other easy-to-grab snacks make up lunch. Leftover spaghetti and meatballs serve as his snack prior to a steak-and-potato dinner. And in between all those main course meals, he travels a well-carved path to the kitchen to clean me out of whatever I bought at the store the day before.

Relief is finally on the way. In two months' time, Jacob leaves for the United States Air Force. For the foreseeable future, Uncle Sam is responsible for funding my boy's eating habits. Brace yourself for a tax increase, my friend. All I know is that the Cushatt family grocery budget is about to drop by at least a third. Thank the Lord in heaven.

I find it fascinating that while our flesh-and-bone bodies require constant sustenance—some of us more than others—God didn't have to create us to need food. He could've created self-sustaining bodies. Or he could've made us like the trees and flowers, able to pull up what we need from our feet while standing in the sun.

Alas, from conception, God made us hungry. At first, we need the nourishment of a mother, connected as we are by umbilical cord, fed by the blood and fluid of another until we take our first breath.

As we grow, our fight against hunger gets more complicated. No longer is food readily at our disposal. We must ask for it, cry for it, plead for it. Then, as we age, we must work for it, purchase it, and prepare it. We are ruled by our hunger every single day.

Perhaps our physical hunger isn't only a chronic problem needing a constant solution. Perhaps our physical hunger is a God-designed hint at a deeper, more serious hunger: a craving of the soul.

I find it's easier to think of breakfast, lunch, and dinner than to pay attention to my soul's longing for a spiritual filling. I'm more accustomed to sitting down throughout the day for a meal or a snack than setting aside time to connect with someone I can't see or touch. I tend to push the deeper hunger aside or satisfy it with lesser foods. A phone call. An hour on social media. Brainless television-watching. Quick fixes, but foolish ones. Substitutions never satisfy.

As a newborn craves a mother's milk, a soul craves the Father's food. I feel it when I watch my child struggle and can't do anything to solve it. I feel the tug of something far bigger than me, a God who wants me to bring my aching heart and child to Him. I feel it when marriage proves to be far more work than reward, when conflict slithers into a conversation and seventeen years of relationship fly out the window. In those lonely moments, I feel Jesus calling me to Him: *I can fill your heart, soothe your wounds. Do you trust Me?*

How about you? Does your gut ache for something more satisfying than your daily routines and relationships? Do you long for something richer than the feast of your current life?

This isn't a flaw needing a human fix. It's a design needing a divine fill.

The Father has promised to fill you with food you can't fathom, a feast on His presence and promises that will make all your lesser attempts at soul satisfaction seem like fool's play. Don't resent the hunger. Slow down enough to recognize it. See your hunger as an invitation to dine. Then seize the moment to find your heart's deepest satisfaction in Him.

Day 16

Oh that we would hunger to be filled with the Word of God; for there is no greater armor, no greater strength, no greater assurance that He is with us, and in us, when we go forth in battle equipped and nourished by His instruction and determined to stand firm on His promises.

—Billy Graham[6]

Who Am I?

What, exactly, is your soul hungry for? Don't rush past this. Consider what you most long for. Is it recognition? Rest from the constant striving? Forgiveness for a mistake? Freedom from a nagging sin? For example, today my soul hunger looks like an aching to be understood. Whatever your heart hungers for most of all, write it down or say it out loud. Then ask your Father to fill it.

Day 17

I Am *Weak*

My grace is sufficient for you, for my power is made perfect in weakness.
—2 Corinthians 12:9

"You're strong, Mom."

My fourteen-year-old announced this over our breakfast cereal. Froot Loops. Definitely not Wheaties. It was a surprising comment for my son to make, considering my bed head, bleary eyes, and two-handed grip on the coffee mug.

I raised both eyebrows in protest. He continued, convinced.

"I mean it, Mom. The only person stronger than you is Jesus." He paused, then added, "And Chuck Norris."

There you have it. On the strength scale, even without Wheaties, I rank right after Jesus and Chuck Norris. I don't mind being third place to those two. Seems only fair, considering one saved the world and the other can whup me on the Total Gym.

I love that my son thinks I'm strong. Love that he feels confident, safe, and secure with his "strong" mama.

But the woman gripping her coffee mug at six in the morning knows otherwise.

Day 17

I am anything but strong. I try to be positive and put on a confident front. I swallow and smile even on the bad days so as not to burden anyone with my worries and fears. But inside, where I wrestle with all the questions and unknowns of life, I'm afraid and so very weak. Dare I say fragile?

Fear is the gap in my armor. Fear is what the enemy uses to maim and cripple me. Fear about my children and their choices. Fear about my health and life expectancy. Fear about my overwhelming to-do list and whether I'll be able to manage it. Fear about my past and my future. Fear about . . .

You get the idea. My fear list is long. And the more I catalog my lackings, to-do's, and worries, the more I feel fear gathering like a storm cloud.

What if . . .?

Depending on the day, different words fill in the blank. On the other side of the question mark sits me, weak and worried. Anything but strong.

Froot Loops, baby. Not Wheaties.

How about you? Do you rank up there with Jesus and Chuck Norris? Or are you like me, a struggler who more often feels weak than strong?

When I read the Bible, only a handful of characters stand out to me as the Chuck Norris type. Abraham. Moses, for the most part. And Paul.

As my son would say, Paul is a boss. He's tough, bold, and fierce enough to endure a lengthy list of persecutions: "Three times I was beaten with rods, once I was pelted with stones, three times I was shipwrecked, I spent a night and a day in the open sea, I have been constantly on the move. I have been in danger from rivers, in danger from bandits, in danger from my fellow Jews, in danger from Gentiles; in danger in the city, in danger in the country, in danger at sea; and in danger from false believers. I have labored and toiled and have often gone without sleep; I have known hunger and thirst and have often gone without food; I have been cold and naked" (2 Cor. 11:25–27).

Like I said, a boss. Who else could endure so much and still be standing? Even with this show of physical and mental strength, however, he counts himself one of us, the weak: "Who is weak, and I do not feel weak? Who is led into sin, and I do not inwardly burn?" (2 Cor. 11:29).

Turns out, Paul wasn't all that different from us. He put on a good front, tried to maintain a positive attitude. But the worries and fears and terrors of this life could overwhelm even a superhero like Paul.

Still, he pressed on. He continued, bold, courageous, and confident, because he understood a surprising truth: weakness is the best platform for God's strength.

Self-sufficiency displays nothing of God's power. Dependency, however, sets the stage for strength to shine. Like wind allows a boat to sail, weakness allows the glory of God to move. This is how Paul could endure in exhausting circumstances.

He believed the strength of God would not fail him.

When God looks at our weakness, our moments of fear and worry and failure, He doesn't shake His head in disappointment and shame. He sees a man or woman dependent on His strength to come in and save the day. Like Paul, we can "delight in weaknesses, in insults, in hardships, in persecutions, in difficulties" (2 Cor. 12:10). How? By choosing to believe it, even when we don't feel it.

After my son's cereal pronouncement, I asked him why he saw me as strong.

"Because you don't give up, Mom. No matter what gets you down, you keep going."

Weak, but banking on God to show up. I'd almost forgotten.

Strength isn't stamina. It's refusing to quit when you have none.

In a word—it's Jesus. The only reason to get back up and keep going is because we believe the one who goes with us will not fail us. We're not self-sufficient. We're Jesus dependent. Day after weary day.

No matter what is sapping your strength or causing you to curl up on the floor exhausted, turn your attention from what you lack toward what He can give.

For when you are weak, He is—you are—strong.

Even without your Wheaties.

You say—but God can never have called me to this, I am too unworthy, it can't mean me. It does mean you, and the weaker and feebler you are, the better.

—Oswald Chambers, *My Utmost for His Highest*

Who Am I?

Consider your various roles. Where do you feel strong? In which roles do you feel the most capable? Second (this question might be easier), where do you feel ill-equipped, overwhelmed, and weak? Now consider this: God's grace is sufficient for both lists. For the roles in which you feel capable and the roles in which you feel weak. Believe His strength will not fail. Say it out loud: "Today, right now, God's grace and strength are sufficient for . . ."

Day 18

I Am Heard

Then you will call on me and come and pray to me, and I will listen to you.

—Jeremiah 29:12

"You're not listening to me."

I cringed at my son's words. He was right. I wasn't listening. Moments before, he'd asked to talk to me. I don't remember what kept me distracted, proof that whatever occupied my attention wasn't all that important. Whether it was washing the dinner dishes, putting a load of laundry in the washing machine, or—to my shame—checking my phone, it doesn't really matter. I allowed the trivial to keep me from the significant. In all my self-important busyness, I hadn't slowed enough to look my son in the eye and listen to what mattered so much to him.

With his honest rebuke, I stopped, embarrassed. Putting aside whatever lesser task had captured my attention, I apologized and promised to listen.

Of course, it wasn't the last time I fumbled in this regard. How many times do I allow myself to become so preoccupied with my to-do's that I miss the people right in front of me?

Perhaps this is why I struggle to believe that the Creator of the Universe slows His planet-spinning to listen to me. If my dishes and laundry and cell phone require so much of my attention, how much more an earth filled with billions of people with needs far greater than mine? Poverty, disease, famine, war. Need I go on? God has His hands full with to-do's. It's incomprehensible that He'd stop long enough to hear me.

King David and other psalmists often cried out with prayers similar to my own. Like me, their circumstances made them desperate to know their tears and pleas were heard by the only one who could relieve them:

- "Hear me, Lord, my plea is just; listen to my cry. Hear my prayer" (Ps. 17:1).
- "Answer me when I call to you, my righteous God. Give me relief from my distress; be merciful to me and hear my prayer" (Ps. 4:1).
- "Look on me and answer, LORD my God. Give light to my eyes, or I will sleep in death" (Ps. 13:3).
- "I am worn out calling for help; my throat is parched. My eyes fail, looking for my God" (Ps. 69:3).

Sound familiar? I've filled journal pages with similar sentiments. At times, these writers even questioned God's presence, assuming their unrelieved suffering was evidence of God's absence: "My God, my God, why have you forsaken me? Why are you so far from saving me, so far from my cries of anguish? My God, I cry out by day, but you do not answer, by night, but I find no rest" (Ps. 22:1–2).

One of my earliest memories is an answered prayer. I couldn't have been more than five years old at the time. A favorite aunt and uncle came into town for a visit—a single night, as I recall. I loved spending time with them and savored every moment. Until my dad sent me to bed. Devastated, I responded by throwing a Hollywood-worthy fit. But in all my theatrics, I forgot to say goodbye to my aunt and uncle. This didn't occur to me until I'd turned off the bedroom light and crawled into bed. There, crying tears of regret into my pillow, I prayed for God to give me a second chance.

Minutes later, the bedroom door cracked open and my uncle came in to say goodnight. The moment lasted only long enough for me to say goodbye, but the impact lasted for years. God heard me. What mattered to me mattered to Him.

And yet, many times since, in spite of my bent knees and begging, bigger prayers seem to have been ignored. And yet, even when one prayer remains unanswered, other prayers are clearly heard. It is then that God's nearness shows up in ways I never expected.

On one particularly difficult day, a month or two after my recent cancer treatment ended, I wrote the following words in my journal: "God, it's tough coming to terms with this 'new me.' I miss my old life, the healthy and strong version of me. What are You up to? How will You use this? I need to see some greater good and purpose. Otherwise, it's just senseless loss, meaningless. God, help me to see You today! Help me to see You working."

A modern-day psalm, you could say. An honest revelation of a woman's spiritual struggle in the face of pain.

Less than an hour later, an email from Jonathan, a stranger halfway across the world in Italy, landed in my inbox: "You know how they always say that you might always find ways through your story to help those who are going through similar situations? Today I listened to you tell your story. It's uncanny how similar our paths have been. . . . I do not know how you are doing right now, but I want you to know that God is still using you, sometimes in uncanny ways. Your suffering is not in vain, and regardless of what lies in between, we have a certain outcome because we believe the God who can be trusted beyond a doubt. . . . In the meantime, as you wait on God, keep looking for that daily manna. I thank God for allowing our paths to cross in such a significant way, even if we live thousands of miles apart."

Day 18

Does the Creator of the Universe hear the prayers of His creation? Yes, He does.

I can't explain the resolution of some prayers and the prolonged ache of others. But I know He hears me, even as my prayers mingle with multitudes of others. Including yours. Unlike me, the Father will never be distracted.

Trust that He hears you, even when it seems otherwise. Ask Him to reveal His activity and presence, to reassure you of His listening ear and tender concern. And then claim, with confidence, "God has surely listened and has heard my prayer" (Ps. 66:19).

It is not objective proof of God's existence that we want but, whether we use religious language for it or not, the experience of God's presence. That is the miracle that we are really after. And that is also, I think, the miracle that we really get.

—FREDERICK BUECHNER, *THE MAGNIFICENT DEFEAT*

Who Am I?

In a moment of difficulty, it's easy to forget God's many times of deliverance. The dark quickly obscures the light, and we fail to remember how often we've known God's nearness and response. Do you believe God hears you? One of the best ways to build up your confidence in God's faithfulness for the future is by keeping record of His prior faithfulness. Whether in a formal journal, a digital document, or an inexpensive spiral notebook, catalogue those moments when it was clear God heard your prayers and responded. Record the date and details so you will not forget.

Day 19

I Am Received

> *I will heal their waywardness and love them freely, for my anger has turned away from them. I will be like the dew to Israel; he will blossom like a lily. Like a cedar of Lebanon he will send down his roots.*
>
> — *Hosea 14:4–5*

From my earliest memory, I loved Jesus. Which is why I never dreamed a day would come when I'd walk away from Him.

My falling out of love with my faith wasn't a flippant decision. It came as a result of prolonged disappointment and pain. After a lifetime of praying for a godly husband and family, I ended up as a twenty-seven-year-old divorced mother of an infant. This wasn't the disappointment of plans falling through. This was the crashing down of everything I'd once prayed for and dreamed of.

Those who have endured a similar wrecking understand something of my deep confusion. I'd been faithful, followed Jesus my whole life. How could God allow me to end up broken and alone? Hadn't I given my life to Him? Wasn't I serving Him in ministry? Didn't my position as child of God afford me some kind of bubble protecting me from calamity? I couldn't reconcile the God of my innocent childhood with the God who seemed silent through the ripping apart of my adulthood.

In the absence of answers, I wanted nothing to do with Him. I couldn't trust a God who abandoned me in my moment of greatest need. I couldn't put my heart in the hands of someone who seemed fickle at best, cruel at worst. If He couldn't grant me an answer to the one prayer I'd prayed more than any other, He must not love me as much as He claimed.

Thus began a bitter season of despair. I avoided church and avoided those who went to church. I buried my pain behind an impenetrable cement exterior, unwilling to allow myself to be duped into another false hope. Before I closed my Bible for a season that lasted about a year, I remember reading, with clenched fists and angry tears, Paul's words in Romans: "we also glory in our sufferings, because we know that suffering produces perseverance; perseverance, character; and character, hope. And hope does not put us to shame, because God's love has been poured out into our hearts through the Holy Spirit, who has been given to us" (Rom. 5:3–5).

What?! I wanted to scream. *Hope* does *disappoint!* My life was proof of that. Every hope I'd once held had been dashed.

The months that followed my descent into despair were some of the darkest I'd ever experienced. In my bitterness, I bristled like a porcupine, my immature effort to resist relationship and thus keep more pain away. In the process, I discovered a more powerful wound: isolation.

Life without God was equally as painful as life with God. But life without God was absent of relief.

My confusion crescendoed on a dark night while I lay awake, staring at the ceiling, my infant son in the other room. Lonely and afraid, I finally admitted my desperation in the first real prayer I'd prayed in far too long: *God, I don't understand You! I don't understand why You'd allow me to experience so much loss. But I need You more than I need to understand. Please don't leave me!*

This was my turning point, the moment when I packed up my bags and returned to a place of faith, like a prodigal desperate for home. It wasn't a clean faith, a faith without questions. But it was a real faith, built on the awareness of my need for God even when I couldn't make sense of Him.

You'd think God would hesitate to receive such a rebellious child back. I'd shaken my fist at Him, ignored the many ways He'd delivered. I'd chosen to focus on the one situation He didn't fix.

For the love of mercy, rather than shut the door on me, Jesus threw it open wide. He didn't love me any less as a result of my doubt. Instead, He offered forgiveness and grace and a safe place to heal.

Faith is often messy and riddled with questions. It's a complicated journey, one further complicated by pain. If you question your faith and struggle to understand this God you can't fathom, be assured you are not alone. From the beginning, humankind has wrestled with the complexities of a hard life and a loving God. The good news is God already knows your questions. He also knows how your heart longs to believe and trust, even in your doubt.

Rather than walk away from your faith, ask God to build it up, to use your circumstances to deepen your belief. And trust His reassurances that your doubts do not dissuade Him. He receives you still, just as you are, and can help you walk through them.

Like a groom who throws a wedding party without the bride's help, we arrive in the circle of His affection simply because He loves us and invited us there. Compassion is His character, kindness His heart. That's good news for you and me. Because no matter how far we fall, as long as we turn back to Him, we will be received.

Day 19

Just as I am, though tossed about
With many a conflict, many a doubt,
Fightings and fears within, without,
O Lamb of God, I come, I come.

Just as I am, poor, wretched, blind;
Sight, riches, healing of the mind,
Yea, all I need in Thee to find,
O Lamb of God, I come, I come.

Just as I am, Thou wilt receive,
Wilt welcome, pardon, cleanse, relieve;
Because Thy promise I believe,
O Lamb of God, I come, I come.

—Charlotte Elliott, "Just As I Am"

Who Am I?

Have you ever experienced a season of walking away from your faith? Or maybe a season of unresolved questions? Are you there now? The admission doesn't surprise the Almighty. The Bible is filled with men and women who struggled with their faith. Although unbelief is a sin, a perfect, untried faith has never been a requirement for salvation. Pray the prayer of the father who pleaded with Jesus for the healing of his son: "I do believe; help me overcome my unbelief!" (Mark 9:24).

Day 20

I Am Clothed

I am going to send you what my Father has promised; but stay in the city until you have been clothed with power from on high.

—Luke 24:49

But the Advocate, the Holy Spirit, whom the Father will send in my name, will teach you all things and will remind you of everything I have said to you.

—John 14:26

Today I'm struggling to write. In spite of my three cups of coffee and one chai tea latte, the words remain out of reach.

Perhaps I should clarify. It's not that I can't write anything. I could, in fact, write about some subjects without any effort. Like the various reasons why dark roast coffee—prepared in a French press for four minutes and topped with enough half-and-half to turn it a lovely shade of butterscotch—is my only beverage of choice before 10:00 a.m.

Or I could wax eloquent about the value of daily reading—primarily historical or classic works—and the way the written word can teach us much about how to live.

Or I could go on and on about the medicinal value of sea salt caramel gelato, eaten by the pint. Only one spoon needed, thank you very much.

Yes, I could entertain you with page upon page on these "lesser" topics without angst. They don't require much, as neither coffee, books, nor gelato carry the weight of the world on their tiny little shoulders. At least not on most days.

But today I sit, mountain sweater wrapped around my shoulders and Macbook Pro propped on my knees, desiring to write words of both challenge and inspiration.

And yet I feel near paralyzed at the thought.

My Bible sits open, its nearness reminding me of its significance. I'm deeply aware of both my desperation for and my ignorance of the sixty-six books within. As much as I love God's Word, I know I'm no pastor. I'm no scholar or theologian. My office walls display no seminary diploma in a shiny brass frame.

I am simply Michele. Ordinary wife and mom from a Denver, Colorado, suburb. I enjoy the Rocky Mountains, long walks at sunrise, and face-to-face conversations. And I make a mean batch of homemade chocolate chip cookies.

Who am I to unpack the mysteries of God and speak with authority on His love and grace? Who am I to wrestle with all I do not understand, to unravel its complexities and deliver both correction and comfort? I am ill-equipped. I'm just an ordinary woman searching for the Most High God.

Is that qualification enough?

Today, I fear it is not.

I'm guessing you have days like that too. Days when you hold the Bible open and turn its onion-skin pages, determined to understand the words, to absorb them and be changed because of them.

But just as soon as you begin to read, you run smack into the sharp awareness of your lack. The mysteries of God are beyond understanding. The depths of His Word impossible to unearth. Even scholars disagree on certain points in the biblical text.

I wonder if the disciples felt the same when they holed up in Jerusalem after Jesus ascended into the heavens. In the weeks before, He had died, risen, and then offered them final words of instruction.

But then the day came when Jesus needed to leave. To head to heaven so God could continue the story He'd been writing since the beginning of time. I wonder if Peter felt an urgency to grab hold of Jesus' robes. I wonder if John tried a last-ditch effort to beg his master to stay. How would they carry on the mission of the gospel without their rabbi leading the way? They were fishermen and tax collectors, Galileans of average backgrounds and trades. They weren't seminary trained or synagogue ordained.

They were ordinary men, desperate to know their God. Was that enough?

Yes. And no.

Which is why Jesus gave them a few final words: "Do not leave Jerusalem, but wait for the gift my Father promised, which you have heard me speak about. For John baptized with water, but in a few days you will be baptized with the Holy Spirit. . . . you will receive power when the Holy Spirit comes on you; and you will be my witnesses in Jerusalem, and in all Judea and Samaria, and to the end of the earth" (Acts 1:4–5, 8).

Were they qualified? Qualifications never entered the equation. Jesus never appeared the least bit interested in their educational or professional resumes. He seemed quite intent to choose those least qualified. And then He promised them they'd be clothed with exactly what they needed to do the job.

The Spirit of God.

It seems the longer we know Jesus and the more we read the Bible, the more we start to buy into this whole idea of education and qualification. There is nothing wrong with a seminary degree. There is certainly great value in becoming a scholar of the Word of God. Every day I give thanks for the men and women who have devoted themselves to the study of biblical and historical texts.

But without the Spirit of God, no amount of study will suffice. No amount of education will unravel the deepest mysteries.

With the Spirit of God, however, even those of us who call ourselves ordinary will discover extraordinary revelation at the feet of Christ Himself.

May the Living God, who is the portion and rest of the saints, make these our carnal minds so spiritual, and our earthly hearts so heavenly, that loving Him, and delighting in Him, may be the work of our lives.

—Richard Baxter, *The Saints' Everlasting Rest*

Who Am I?

It's interesting—and telling—that God chose the common and ordinary as His closest friends and disciples. Knowing our tendency to either rely on our own smarts and skills or gravitate to those who have both, He went for those who had little of which to boast. How does this knowledge change your view of your qualifications for ministry—or lack thereof? Ask God to make you His student, to clothe you with His Spirit and make you hungry to sit at His feet and learn.

Part 3

Covenant

Day 21

I Am *Seen*

And even the very hairs of your head are all numbered.
—Matthew 10:30

He stood well over six feet tall, a towering figure of a man, especially to my petite sixth-grade self. Beyond his height, his every physical detail was—how should I say?—breathtaking. Even at twelve years old, I knew my sixth-grade teacher was no ordinary man. Tanned skin, dark hair, killer smile.

Be still my heart.

It wasn't so much his handsomeness that drew me to him. Although, *hello.* Truth is I became a forever Mr. Cantrell fan for a different reason.

For the prior five years of grade school, I'd felt invisible. A no-name girl who'd attended three different schools and drifted in and out of classrooms. I did my schoolwork without fanfare, my awkwardness overshadowing any intelligence or personality prepped to bloom. I was an insecure, invisible girl in an Illinois school filled with hundreds of louder, smarter, cuter kids.

But then, sixth grade. And a cute science teacher named Mr. Cantrell.

Within the first few weeks of class, during one of his always-entertaining teaching sessions, he simply asked a question. Then, after searching the faces of his students, his eyes and smile landed on me.

"Michele."

I must've gaped, because he grinned in response.

"Yes, you. What do you think?"

I swear he winked at me, as if we shared a secret. That's all it took.

In that moment, with this unremarkable exchange of words, the twelve-year-old me came alive. It was as if he knew I held the answer, believed me capable of great things. As if an electric current had traveled from him to me, I felt alive with his confidence. For the first time in my life, I believed in me. No longer invisible, no longer ignored.

Instead, *seen.*

He continued calling me out of hiding for the rest of the school year. With each interaction, I grew more comfortable in my own skin. It's one of the few school scenes I still vividly recall. Mr. Cantrell ignited a transformation that changed my story. Simply because he chose to see an invisible twelve-year-old girl.

There's a similar story in the New Testament that has always intrigued me. The details are recorded in both Mark and Luke, although each account spares only a few verses for the story. It's short enough to make me wonder at its inclusion in the biblical canon at all. And yet there it is. Twice.

It's the story of the poor widow. Neither account provides her name, relatives, address, or occupation. This we do know: She'd endured great loss. She had little of value left in this life. And she worshiped God.

On that day, Jesus sat in the temple watching worshipers give their offerings. Before she arrived, the wealthy paraded through, making dramatic show of their generous gifts. Imagine them dropping their coins in the offering one at a time.

Ping! What sacrifice!

Ping! What generosity!

Ping! What devotion to God!

Or not. Jesus didn't appear to be the least bit impressed.

Until the widow arrived with two small coins. Mark says her "very small" offering amounted to a few cents, not enough for the temple treasurer to buy more incense or feed an orphan child. Like pennies on the sidewalk, hardly worth the effort to stoop and pick up.

And yet this is what she brought her God. Everything she had.

And her God noticed.

"Truly I tell you, this poor widow has put more into the treasury than all the others" (Mark 12:43).

After a series of far more extravagant displays of giving, Jesus noticed the small and invisible. A poor and ordinary woman in a crowd of the righteous and wealthy.

I've long been a fan of the underdog. And at Jesus' words in this story, everything in me wants to stand and cheer. *He sees! Jesus sees her!* She matters to Him, both her lack and her love pouring out in a sacrifice most of us will never understand. And if Jesus saw her, then maybe He sees me.

> *Blessed is the nation whose God is the LORD,*
> *the people he chose for his inheritance.*
> *From heaven the LORD looks down*
> *and sees all mankind;*
> *from his dwelling place he watches*
> *all who live on earth.*
>
> —PSALM 33:12–14

> *Though the LORD is exalted, he looks kindly on the lowly;*
> *though lofty, he sees them from afar.*
> *Though I walk in the midst of trouble,*
> *you preserve my life.*
>
> —PSALM 138:6–7

Day 21

The God of the universe, the one who set the stars and sun in the sky, the one who knows the workings of every cell of my body and sparks the grand and glorious display of His creation, sees me. And He sees you.

Eventually sixth grade ended and middle school began. I lost track of Mr. Cantrell, and to this day I don't know where he is or whether he would even remember the awkward, invisible girl from his sixth-grade science class.

But this I do know: I will never outgrow my place in God's classroom. He's the most breathtaking person in the room. I'm smitten. And in an ocean of other names and faces, He sees me.

"Let not your heart be troubled," His tender word I hear,
And resting on His goodness, I lose my doubts and fears;
Though by the path He leadeth, but one step I may see;
His eye is on the sparrow, and I know He watches me.

—Civilla D. Martin, "His Eye Is on the Sparrow"

Who Am I?

In Exodus 4:31, we see the response of the Israelites when they realize God has seen their suffering, *seen them.* After four hundred years of feeling invisible, they discover that God not only sees them and hears their prayers but also feels deep compassion for them in their grief. So they fall on the ground and worship. A beautiful response to an incomparable gift. Do you believe God sees you? Your answer just might impact the sweetness of your worship.

Day 22

I Am Accepted

The Father himself loves you because you have loved me and have believed that I came from God.

—John 16:27

The trip was to be a reunion of sorts, a gathering of peers from around the country to meet at a well-known conference. I'd planned the trip for months and counted down the days in sweet anticipation. Although some work would be involved, it was a girls' weekend away, a much-needed investment in self-care. I dreamed of heartfelt conversations with old friends and exciting connections with new ones. Although I'd miss my family, I knew I needed this. For them and for me.

Ready, I boarded the plane, stashed my carry-on below the seat in front of me. With my chai latte in one hand and a new book in the other, I settled in for a soul-filling. I couldn't wait.

One day into the conference, however, and I knew I'd been mistaken. Instead of a soul-filling getaway, it was turning out to be a soul-sucking experience watching my confidence drain. In a place filled with the sounds of relationship, I was invisible. A dozen or more women whose names I knew and who knew my own laughed and cried and savored the gift of time shared. Only they did it with each other and without me.

Like a marble in a pinball game, I ricocheted from person to person, trying to find a place at their tables, attempting to squeeze into their conversations.

It didn't work. The more I tried, the tighter they circled. While they held on to each other, I sat alone.

What's wrong with me? I wondered.

This was the question that plagued me day after day throughout the conference. These were beautiful women, full of faith and wisdom and life. I ached to be part of their lifegiving circle, but there seemed to be no room in it for me. After a couple of days, my self-esteem was in shreds.

I called my husband, needing his reassurance.

"You have a place, Michele. Here, with me." I relished his love. Still, the sting of rejection remained.

After the conference ended, I returned to the airport, bruised and disappointed. I counted down the minutes and seconds until departure, desperate for the shield of home. My flight couldn't leave fast enough.

But something changed once the plane was in the air. Conviction replaced rejection. During the conference, I'd spent my best self in an effort to be seen and accepted, trying to hide my flaws and be good enough.

But as I strained to find my seat at old friends' tables, I ignored countless others looking for a seat of their own.

Beyond the small group of women I tried to infiltrate, hundreds more gathered at the conference. Rather than see their faces and stories, I remained consumed by my own. In the end, I left frustrated that I was unable to build friendships with those I already knew, but convicted that I was also unwilling to spark a connection with those I didn't.

Embarrassed, I suspected the latter was a far greater tragedy.

The desire to feel accepted isn't unique to me. There's a story in the Old Testament about a boy who, likewise, couldn't find his place.

Although born a prince, the son of King David's best friend, Jonathan, Mephibosheth endured a crippling accident that left him hiding in isolation. You'd think being physically disabled would make it impossible to be invisible. The thing you want most to hide is the very reason people can't take their eyes off you. But often we can't see the person behind their obvious flaws.

And so it was for Mephibosheth until Kind David started looking for the one he missed, the son of his friend Jonathan. Rather than having eyes only for the popular crowd, King David searched for someone lost who needed to be found. And when he found him, he did something about it: "Mephibosheth . . . will always eat at my table" (2 Sam. 9:10).

The words of a king to the heart of an outcast. Just like that, Mephibosheth found his place. It was settled.

We all want to be accepted by those we admire. So we work hard to show our best selves and hide our limp. Anxious to fit in, we move from one circle to another, trying to find our place and searching for an empty chair. But there's a problem: it's the wrong chair.

The King already has a place with your name on it. And one with mine. He doesn't have eyes for the popular. Instead, He looks for the lost needing to be found. And when He finds you and me, He says, *You will always eat at My table.*

I'm tired of spending my best self to find a chair at a lesser table. I have a place, established and firm. So do you. We no longer need to struggle and strain to squeeze into relationships. That isn't where we're supposed to pull up a chair anyway.

Instead, as we love and lead, we can settle into the one chair made especially for us. Secure, once and for all. Only then will we have eyes for the invisible. Let's not let our insecurity blind us to opportunity. If we allow ourselves to be consumed with our own needs, we'll miss the many needs around us. And often, in the meeting of another's need, we find our needs cured.

Day 22

In a world of Mephibosheths, I want my voice to be David's and my table filled with the lost. Crippled misfits called by a King. Accepted just as we are. Including both me and you.

There was only one sort of person whom the Lord Jesus did not accept when He said, "Come." They are the ones who said to Him, "Yes, here I am, Jesus, and I'm very good and very virtuous." . . . To them the Lord Jesus said, "Are you very virtuous? Then I am sorry, but I can't help you."

—Corrie ten Boom, *I Stand At the Door and Knock*

Who Am I?

In this world of fickle friendship, it's easy to forget that we have a permanent seat at God's table. Too often we seek lesser chairs, looking for shallow approvals and satisfactions. In spite of the world's promises, human acceptance will never be enough. First, contemplate your pursuit of lesser positions. Where are you nearly desperate for acceptance? Is it time to let it go? Second, consider those you may have overlooked in your pursuit of your place. Today ask God to give you insight and courage to take one step toward someone who needs to know they have a place at the King's table.

Day 23

I Am Wanted

I will not leave you as orphans; I will come to you.
—John 14:18

The night held magic. I knew it before the sixteen-year old boy standing next to me reached for my hand.

Although we went to the same high school, I couldn't believe it when he asked me out. He was an athlete, part of the popular crowd. I was completely average, an insecure academic who didn't have the looks or charm or sass to be part of any elite group.

So when he asked me to dinner, I fell all over myself saying yes. Clearly, my high school luck was changing.

I remember nothing about the date except for its ending. After driving us back to my parents' house, he grabbed my hand and took me outside for a walk.

The moon and stars filled the fall sky like scattered shards of crystal. The evening was just cool enough to require a light jacket, but nothing more. Idyllic conditions for a romantic, hand-holding walk. Everything about the night seemed perfect. Which is why I didn't balk when he pulled me to a stop and leaned in. His lips touched mine in an explosion of adolescent fireworks.

Day 23

My first kiss.

Magic. In seconds, I went from unwanted to wanted, average to extraordinary. I floated like a balloon on a string held in his hand as he walked me back home.

The magic of the moment carried over to the next morning. Someone liked me! After years of girlish longing, it felt amazing to be wanted. Little did I know, the dream wouldn't last. Too soon, the magic proved nothing but an illusion.

The truth became clear when I arrived at school. Within seconds, the girl sitting next to me in class said words that stopped me cold: "Something looks different about you today, Michele. Like something happened last night, for the first time." It wasn't her words as much as the gleam in her eye that gave her away.

She knew.

Heat filled my cheeks. I tried to shrug it off, but even my naive self knew something was amiss. My fears were confirmed when another girl—someone I'd known for most of my life—said something similar. Throughout the day, more smirks and comments came my way. Then, when the boy never again acknowledged my existence, reality made itself plain.

The entire thing had been a setup. A sham. A few weeks before, I'd confided to a friend that I'd never been kissed. She spilled my secret to a high school full of unmerciful teenagers. What I thought was magic was merely a popular boy's response to an adolescent dare.

Nothing but a game. He won. I lost.

I lost far more than my first kiss that day. I lost my innocence. I'd been duped, manipulated, and misled. I wasn't wanted; I was used. A prop to propel a teenage boy a little farther up the popularity scale.

As a result, I bought into the belief that the only way I'd ever be wanted is if I worked at it. I needed to put on a good show and put some effort into being worthy.

My experience with human love has, at times, left me jaded and self-protective. I'm afraid to trust love, to lean into it. I'm afraid I'll find myself once again duped and unwanted. And yet the Bible promises God's love can be counted on. Do I trust His sincerity? Do I believe He will not fail me?

There's a story in the Bible about a woman who needed to be noticed by a man. When Ruth's husband died suddenly along with her father-in-law, she became destitute, along with her adored mother-in-law, Naomi. Wanted one day, alone and without resources the next. No spouses, no means of income or provision. Alone.

Until Ruth discovered she had a kinsman, a relative who could assume the role of husband out of respect for his deceased relative.

But it was a long shot. Why would this relative, Boaz, want to give up his independence for a widow and her mother-in-law? An unnecessary burden. And yet Ruth and Naomi both knew it was their only option.

So one night, after the day's work was done, Ruth walked over to the field where Boaz worked. She found him asleep on the threshing floor, likely exhausted from a full day's work, and she curled up at his feet to sleep. As custom dictated, when he awakened to find that Ruth had "thrown herself at his feet" during the night, Boaz had a choice to make: receive her as his wife—and become her kinsman-redeemer—or reject her request. It may seem difficult to understand, but Ruth's life hinged on the whims of one man's wants.

Have you been there? Maybe you're not a woman waiting for a man. Maybe you're simply a person waiting to be wanted. You trusted love once upon a time. But then a rejection or loss. An injustice or betrayal. Something hardened within. Never again would you throw yourself at the feet of anyone. *Never.*

I understand. But I've learned something since that devastating first kiss. Human desire is a flawed echo of a flawless love. While there is merit in romance, it was never meant to be the apex of all love. Instead, it's merely a hint of something far better.

God *is* love. We are wanted by one who plays no games and hides no ulterior motives. His love heals our wounds and soothes our hearts. And when we throw ourselves at His feet, there is no fear of what the morning will bring.

For the morning brings with it the knowledge that we're already wanted.

We're redeemed by the one who holds the power to do the redeeming. Every lesser love is merely child's play.

To know that love is of God and to enter into the secret place leaning upon the arm of the Beloved—this and only this can cast out fear.

—A. W. Tozer, *The Knowledge of the Holy*

Who Am I?

As much as Hollywood and our own fantasies attempt to fool us, human love will always fail us to some degree. It's beautiful at times, no doubt about it. But divine love will always leave human love wanting. Human desire is merely a hint of something greater, even on its best days. Do you have unrealistic expectations of human love? How can the reality of God's desire for you bring healing to your past and current relationships?

Day 24

I Am Welcomed

Come to me, all you who are weary and burdened, and I will give you rest.

—Matthew 11:28

I saw her across the church foyer after Sunday services let out. Diane. A single mom with a special needs son. We'd known each other for years, had once attended a Bible study together. But time had passed and circumstances had changed. In a church our size, it was easy to go months without crossing paths. It had been more than two or three years since Diane and I had last caught up.

You should go talk to her, I thought. *See how she's doing.*

Instead, I headed toward the children's department with my husband to pick up our three kids. As I walked, I started planning lunch. Reminded myself to throw in a load of laundry. Again, thoughts of Diane interrupted.

You really should go back and find her. At least say hi.

I should. Yes, I knew I should. But the problem was I didn't want to. Actually, my *heart* wanted to, my mind and body did not. Instead, I wanted to get in the car and drive home, maybe crawl into bed for a long Sunday afternoon nap. After navigating my own complicated life, I just didn't have the strength to step into hers. I was exhausted. So I went home.

I wish I could say this was a one-time scenario. But how many times has the scene repeated itself? In the grocery store. At the park. Dropping off or picking kids up from school. I run into a familiar face, but rather than engage, I walk away. Not every time, but enough. It's not that I don't care. I'm just too weary with my burdens to throw out the welcome mat for someone else's.

It's too much sometimes, this great sea of human need. Whether it's in the church foyer or on the ten o'clock news, I see desperation everywhere and hardly know how to touch it. Single mothers. Troubled fathers. Homelessness, human trafficking, abused and unwanted refugees. It's an ocean of pain on all sides, including my own. All these obvious needs move me, break me, overwhelm me. I feel helpless, knowing my offerings, whatever they may be, would be far too small. So, I admit, sometimes I'd rather look away and walk away.

To welcome another's suffering means I suffer. And I already have enough of that.

And yet when I went through horrific illness, I had a few faithful friends who stayed close. In spite of my neediness, they pulled up a chair and listened for hours at a time. They let me cry, sleep, even lose my lunch on occasion. They weren't turned off by my pain. Instead, they helped me carry it. In many ways, it saved me.

Others couldn't, of course. In spite of sincere hearts and good intentions, their own pain kept them from touching mine. They stayed away, loving me from a distance, but not able to welcome my broken self into their world.

I understand. Really, I do. The wounds of this world are often far beyond an ordinary human capacity to comfort. So where do we turn when we have no place else to go with our pain? Who can be trusted to stick with us when the struggle is great?

"Come to me, all you who are weary and burdened, and I will give you rest," Jesus said (Matt. 11:28). Jesus had a knack for welcoming the least likely of guests. He didn't require them to clean up, get it together, finish their education, change their language, or even convert to His "religion." Instead, He entered their homes, engaged in conversations. With a sweep of His arm, He wiped the requirements from the table, pulled up a chair, and simply said, "Come. Have a seat. With Me."

He shared dinner with a tax collector no one else wanted near.

He sat down to a lengthy dialogue with a demon-possessed cave dweller.

He chose uneducated fishermen as His closest friends.

He asked a questionable Samaritan woman for a conversation and a drink of water.

A poor widow. A Roman centurion. A cast-out leper. A rejected blind man. I could spend half the day talking about the down-and-outs whom Jesus welcomed. Undeterred by their needs, choices, and circumstances, He leaned in. Engaged. Listened.

And today, if Jesus stood in my church foyer or settled into my living room sofa, He wouldn't shrink from the wide swath of suffering. He'd do something about it.

The same is true for you, you know. Regardless of your bruised and battered soul, Jesus welcomes you without condition.

Come.

Are you weary? Weighed down by your life's story? Overwhelmed by unknowns? Come. We'll carry it together.

This world is not an easy one to weather. We will not always be able to carry another's burdens along with our own. But when we find our rest in Jesus first, we'll have far more strength to welcome the Dianes we meet like He does.

The burden of men was so heavy for God Himself that He had to endure the Cross. God verily bore the burden of men in the body of Jesus Christ. But He bore them as a mother carries her child, as a shepherd enfolds the lost lamb that has been found. God took men upon Himself and they weighted Him to the ground, but God remained with them and they with God.

—Dietrich Bonhoeffer, *Life Together*

Who Am I?

When a need is far greater than our ability to meet it, we tend to shrink back. We doubt our ability to make a difference, and so we ignore what sits right in front of us. Thank heavens, Jesus did the opposite. The size of need didn't deter Him. On the contrary, He moved toward those who needed Him most. Are you weary, burdened, overwhelmed by your life? Jesus' invitation is for you: *Come.* Tell Him your story, share with Him your most private heart. He will give you rest.

Day 25

I Am Rescued

Because he loves me . . . I will rescue him; I will protect him, for he acknowledges my name.

—Psalm 91:14

In a crowd of forty thousand strangers, my five-year-old son disappeared. One moment, he was holding my hand. The next moment, he was gone.

Minutes before, I'd crossed the finish line of my first 10K race. I'd long dreamed of becoming a true runner, otherwise known as someone able to move faster than a crawl without passing out. So as a New Year's resolution, I'd set my sights on a worthy goal: the Bolder Boulder. One of the most famous 10K races in the United States. Held every year on Memorial Day in Boulder, Colorado. I committed to run the entire course.

Thus began my training, otherwise known as self-torture. For months I agonized, pushing myself to go a little farther, a little faster. Eventually, I picked up the pace enough that passersby might have called that thing I was doing a slow jog. All the while, I never took my eyes off my Memorial Day goal.

Only the experience didn't turn out quite like I thought it would. Yes, I ran the entire Bolder Boulder. A total of 6.2 miles in sixty-two minutes. For a first race, I couldn't have been more pleased.

But my feeling of accomplishment vanished as quickly as my son did. Within moments of my crossing the finish line to the welcoming faces of my family, my youngest son let go of my hand. And the sweetness of the moment got swallowed up by his disappearance.

Almost every parent I know has experienced a moment similar to this one. They vanish so quickly, like water slipping through our palms, and we're left standing alone in the shopping mall or grocery store or parking lot, realizing how easily bliss can be swallowed up by fear.

The following fifteen minutes were some of the longest of my life. My husband and I instinctively split up, screaming our son's name into the churning mass of finishers and well-wishers. An impossible task. How were we to find a five-year-old in such a sea of humanity? How would our voices be heard among thousands of others?

By some miracle, we found him. Twenty or thirty yards away, surrounded by strangers, oblivious to both the danger and the distance.

But I knew. As I exhaled in relief, I contemplated, with trembling, how differently it could've turned out. In all, the rescue took fifteen minutes. Yet I would have searched for days and weeks, months and years if necessary. No amount of time would have been too great.

Luke 15 records three short stories that remind me a lot of that day. Jesus tells each story in response to the grumbling religious leaders who turned their noses up at the kind of company He kept. Sinners and criminals and reprobates. People who were no doubt spiritually lost. Individuals who didn't follow all the rules. They were like children. Prone to trouble. Destined to wander.

The first story features a shepherd and his wandering sheep. Stating the obvious, Jesus asks, "Doesn't he leave the ninety-nine in the open country and go after the lost sheep until he finds it?" (Luke 15:4).

The second scene is more intimate, more desperate. After saving up ten silver coins, a woman notices she's lost one. This is 10 percent of her savings, a sizable chunk of her livelihood now gone. She tears her house apart to find it, turning over couch cushions and digging through the washing machine until—at last!—she finds her missing coin. Just as in the case of the shepherd, she invites her friends and throws a party.

The final story is far more emotional than the other two, like the slow but certain crescendo of a symphony nearing its culmination.

A father has two sons. The older is well behaved, follows the rules, and stays close to home. The younger is impetuous, selfish, and immature. He can't see beyond dollar signs and freedom. So he asks for an early inheritance and takes off for parties and personal satisfaction.

This third story is often named the parable of the lost son. But if you look closely, the story is more about the heart of the father than the habits of his boys. In the cases of both the wayward son and the stay-at-home son, the father does all he can to hold his children close. He knows an important truth: You don't have to run away to be lost. The younger son eventually returns home, broken and contrite. And yet the older son—the one who obeyed the rules—still remains distant from the true heart of the father.

Even so. Even with a younger son who blew his father's money and an older son who scorned his father's grace, the father makes it clear he's all about the rescue.

Like an anxious mama who would give her last breath to find a little boy who let go of her hand.

Now let's get personal. Have you ever let go of the Father's hand? Of course you have. So have I. Probably far more than once this past week. Sometimes our wandering looks like rebellion and rejection of everything we know to be right and good. A lie. A betrayal. An affair.

Most of the time, however, our wandering is far less plain. Self-righteousness. Unforgiveness. Apathy. Pride. Like the older son in comparison to the younger, these offenses may appear more acceptable.

But the resulting distance is the same: We slip our hand out of the Father's and attempt to make our way on our own.

But here's the good news, both in our intentional wanderings and our unintentional ones. We have a Father who will turn His house upside down to bring us back to Him. A sheep and a coin have nothing on a beloved child. He will rescue you, and He'll do it with more grace and love than you've ever known.

He has given His life to the cause of rescue. Hands and feet nailed to a cross so we won't fear slipping from His grasp. Ever.

This is the most profound spiritual truth I know: That even when we're most sure that love can't conquer all, it seems to anyway. It goes down into the rat hole with us, in the guise of our friends, and there it swells and comforts. It gives us second winds, third winds, hundredth winds.

—Anne Lamott, *Traveling Mercies*

Who Am I?

You've likely lived long enough to know that rescue doesn't mean God will prevent all pain and hardship. Unexpected life still happens, even when God is in it. No, God doesn't always rescue us *from* harm, but He always rescues us *in* it. (Go ahead and read that again.) How have you seen this truth play out in your life? How can this truth shore up how you see yourself and make you *more* secure?

Day 26

I Am

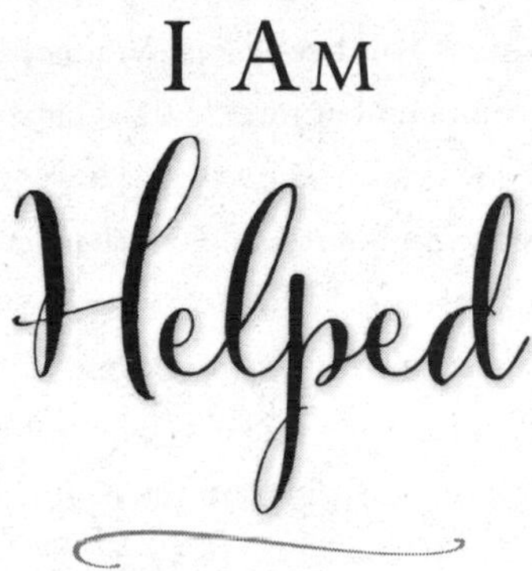

For I, the Lord your God, hold your right hand; it is I who say to you, "Fear not. I am the one who helps you."
—Isaiah 41:13 (ESV)

I didn't want to go.

I had to, I knew. We planned to kick off a conference the next day, and I was one of the leaders and speakers. I dreaded the thought of standing up on a stage and opening my mouth in front of a hundred strangers. I couldn't hide my speech difficulties anymore. Within the first sentence, everyone would hear a lisp, wonder why I talked funny. I didn't want to expose myself to the questions and speculation, didn't want to open the door to hard, painful conversations. I wanted to hide.

But I had a job to do, as much as I didn't want to do it.

Help, God. Please. Help me.

Help came, in the most unusual way.

I met her less than twenty-four hours after my arrival. Paula. A hotel employee responsible for serving our team lunch before the conference began. She didn't say much during our meeting, content to refill our glasses and remove our plates. Although I noticed her, I didn't think much about her.

Until our meeting ended and we started to clear out of the room.

That's when she stopped me on my way out the door. She started by asking me if my lunch had been okay. She'd noticed I hadn't eaten much, and a fellow team member mentioned in passing that I'd recently recovered from significant cancer surgery. She lowered her voice, paused, and then dropped her bomb: "I just found out I have cancer. Breast cancer. I meet with my oncologist for the first time tomorrow."

Just that fast, two strangers became friends. What followed over the next few moments included a beautiful, honest exchange of stories. Then came her questions, starting with the big one: "How did you get through it?"

I didn't know whether she claimed any faith or belief in God. No matter. She asked an honest question, and I gave her an honest answer.

"God. I believe God is real, and He loves you and me more than we know. He is the one who helped me through. I wouldn't have made it without my faith in Him."

The minute the words left my mouth, I knew why I was at the conference.

To help a woman in the middle of a hard thing know the love of a real God.

And at the same time, to rediscover God's help for me.

The writer of Psalm 46:1 said these words: "God is our refuge and strength, an ever-present help in trouble."

Right here, right now, God is able and willing to help us walk through the hard thing. For me that day, it involved standing up on a stage again and speaking to an audience. For Paula, it was walking into an oncologist's office for the first time. And as only God can do, He helped both of us by weaving our similar stories together in a divinely crafted moment.

My good friend Becky is in one of those wretched waiting spaces, the kind that could dramatically impact her life by either its resolution or lack thereof. From the darkness of her hard place, she asked this question: "What lessons have you learned in life's waiting room? How do you survive the tension? What does God teach us here?"

Ugh. I know a thing or two about life's waiting room. About sitting in a hard place and waiting for help to come.

It's painful, exhausting, infuriating, [insert expletive here].

Still. I must concede waiting spaces are ripe for lesson learning, including revelations like

- How little control we have.
- How much control we want.
- How necessary waiting spaces are for building up our faith.

I know, I know. I threw up a little while writing those last words.

But here's the deal: It's one thing to talk about faith in a God who comes to our rescue, another to live as if you're banking on it. Like it or not, we humans rely an awful lot on our ability to control and manage circumstances. Even worry is an effort to control.

But real faith is a letting go. A releasing of the what-if's when everything in you wants to tighten your grip. It's allowing yourself to free fall into the unknown because you have absolute confidence that waiting at the other end are arms big enough to catch you, help you, and make you whole.

Easy to write, not easy to live. But the payout is peace.

Let my people go, became God's rallying cry, that they might worship me. At the heart of liberty—of being let go—is worship. But at the heart of worship is rest—a stopping from all work, all worry, all scheming, all fleeing—to stand amazed and thankful before God and his work. There can be no real worship without true rest.

—Mark Buchanan, *The Rest of God*

Day 26

Who Am I?

What hard thing are you up against? Many times, we determine to roll up our sleeves and dig in. We think if we work hard enough, we can make the challenges go away. But many times, our efforts do little to change our circumstances and, instead, fool us into thinking we're in control. It's not so much about our strength and ability to get through as it is about God's ever-present help regardless of what may come. How can you lean less on yourself and more on Him in the middle of your hard thing?

Day 27

I AM *Marked*

Can a mother forget the baby at her breast and have no compassion on the child she has borne? Though she may forget, I will not forget you! See, I have engraved you on the palms of my hands.

—ISAIAH 49:15–16

He left it on my desk, right before he walked out the door for another day of kindergarten. A large, eleven-by-seventeen creation with the letters of his name printed in thick red and black marker. He wanted to leave his mark where I wouldn't miss it. As if he feared I'd forget about him while he was gone.

It has been nearly five years since he joined our family, a little boy from a hard background enveloped into a family determined to make him feel safe, loved. Within a month of his arrival, we nicknamed him Radar. Because from the moment he wakes up until his head hits the pillow at night, he's pinging the world with constant reminders that he exists.

Some days he does this by following his dad from room to room, afraid to let him leave his sight, fearing he might be left behind. Other days—most days—he says "I love you" a hundred times, ping after ping from an eight-year-old desperate for a hundred "I love you's" in return.

Day 27

It's been a struggle for me, his never-assuaged neediness. I understand the hurt behind it, the attachment wounds that fuel his fear and insecurity. But the depth of his void can be overwhelming. I can hold his face in my hands, look deep into his brown eyes, and offer my most earnest "I love you." But like a black hole that swallows every hint at light, five minutes later he's back, needing more.

Ping! Ping! Ping!

I shake my head and wonder, What will it take to fill his heart, once and for all? I don't know. I just don't know. And so I pray that the God who sees this boy's deepest needs will, somehow, heal him.

Today, as I think of his eleven-by-seventeen art, I see how very much like me he is. Like all of us. We too have fearsome black holes in need of filling. We too ping the world with our presence, asking for reassurance that we matter.

Some days it looks like too many hours online, back-to-back coffee dates, or a nagging critical attitude. But sometimes our radar pings aren't so pretty. Hiding a deep hole, we pout and throw tantrums of adult-sized proportions. We complain, attack, accuse, overreact, and throw ourselves at near strangers, asking them to follow us, friend us, and value our offerings. Behind the meltdown, our need is the same:

- Do you see me?
- Do I matter?
- Don't forget I'm here!

But a thousand radar pings aren't going to fill our void. They might afford us a few quick affirmations or momentary sympathies. But eventually the black hole of need swallows up even the best attempts to make us feel loved.

To know we matter comes from within, not without. It's not an external filling, worldly affirmations collected one Facebook friend and coffee date at a time. Significance isn't an external number but an internal assurance. My value—your value—isn't subject to public scrutiny or a vote. It's not based on that painful criticism you received or the long history of mistakes you've made. And it's not sourced in the "I love you's" you solicit or the accolades you merit.

It's based not on anything you do but on the fact that *you are*.

"I have engraved you on the palms of my hands," God says (Isa. 49:16). He tattoos your existence in this world—*your name*—on His very self. No need to leave an eleven-by-seventeen reminder of your presence. No fear He'll forget you once He gets busy with the tasks of the day.

You are His. Marked in red marker on His hands. He can no more remove you from His thoughts than He can separate His arm from His body.

God's personal love is the putty that fills our cracks. When we know our value to God and secure our lives on that truth, one hundred "I love you's" don't disappear into a black hole of need. They simply add to what the one who made us already said is true.

It won't be easy to live marked by the unfailing love of God. One moment you'll feel all warm and fuzzy with it, the next you'll doubt it. It's far easier to follow other people around, waiting and hoping to be loved.

But never forget: Only God's love is a sure thing. Only God's love marks us in permanent ink and never rubs off. We're loved, wanted, and never, ever forgotten.

The maker of the stars would rather die for you than live without you. And that is a fact. So if you need to brag, brag about that.

—Max Lucado, *Traveling Light*

Day 27

Who Am I?

The need to belong is basic to the human experience. We need to know that we're seen and that we matter. In the absence of belonging, we ping the world for reassurance. For the next twenty-four hours, consider how you ping your world for reassurance. Think about the various ways you reach for affirmation in your relationships and circumstances, confirmation of your belonging. Then begin to build a new pattern of "following God around the house." Lean on Him first for your reassurance, knowing you're already marked as His. As a reminder, you might want to write the word "Loved" in red marker on your right hand.

Day 28

I Am Renamed

The one who is victorious I will make a pillar in the temple of my God. Never again will they leave it. I will write on them the name of my God and the name of the city of my God, the new Jerusalem, which is coming down out of heaven from my God; and I will also write on them my new name.

—Revelation 3:12

Call me antiquated or old school, I don't care. Adopting my husband's last name might've been my favorite part of getting married.

Engaged at twenty years old, I spent an inordinate amount of time practicing my new last name, both written and verbal. I doodled it in notebooks and walked through my parents' house saying it out loud. I imagined writing checks with my new name, answering to my new name, sending letters with my new name. I even printed special return-address labels, excited as I was about my new marriage.

I never dreamed my new name wouldn't last. And when my husband left after six years of marriage, I had to wear a name I never wanted to claim: divorced.

For more than a decade, this name plagued me. Embarrassed, I did everything I could to hide the truth from those I met. At church, parties, and community gatherings, I pretended I was a normal twentysomething, unmarred by a broken marriage. Inevitably, the subject of family came up. They asked their questions in innocence, simply making conversation. They didn't realize the gaping wound each question opened in me: "Are you married? How many children do you have? Where's your husband?"

I'm pretty sure my face flushed with each inquiry. Unable to avoid the truth, I hung my head and delivered an honest reply, trying to swallow my shame as I bounced my two-year-old on my hip.

"No, I'm not married. I'm divorced."

Awkward silence always followed my admission. Nobody knows what to say to a young, divorced mother. I interpreted their silence as judgment, insecure as I was. Perhaps my assumption was accurate, perhaps not. But it didn't matter. I judged myself.

The label followed me well into my second marriage, when schoolteachers noticed one of my children had a different last name than the others. And at sporting events, when former spouses showed up, creating a complicated family drama. Not to mention countless awkward explanations to old friends who hadn't yet heard of my first marriage's demise.

Divorced. Divorced. Divorced.

I imagined the words being whispered behind my back as friends and family struggled to make sense of this unexpected turn of events. I'd failed at the one thing I needed to get right—marriage and family. And no matter how much I loved my new husband and children, we'd never be able to recreate the traditional family we'd lost.

As time passed, the name grew unbearably heavy, stifling. Until I finally realized I didn't have to wear a label of shame anymore.

"You will be called by a new name that the mouth of the LORD will bestow. You will be a crown of splendor in the LORD's hand, a royal diadem in the hand of your God" (Isa. 62:2–3).

Divorce was part of my story. But it couldn't dictate the future of my family unless I let it. Divorce is a dot on the timeline of my life, a dot that has impacted multiple other dots, no doubt about it. But a dot just the same.

I am not divorce.

I am not failure.

I'm a reflection of the life and presence of Christ. I carry His name, I wear His covering, I walk in His grace and mercy and forgiveness. My name has been established by the God who claims me as His own. I'm His.

A day is coming, promises the book of Revelation, when our knight on a white horse will ride in to exact both judgment and mercy upon this earth. When that day comes, He will bestow on you and me a new name, His name. All the other names and labels we've lugged around for a lifetime will be swallowed up by a bigger and better one.

No more shame. No more need to hide. No more labels we can't shed.

Instead of broken, rebuilt.

Instead of lost, found.

Instead of unwanted, chosen.

Instead of unmarried, married to the Most High.

The weight of every lesser name we've carried will be lifted from our shoulders, even as the one who calls us His own places a crown on our heads. As a groom calls his bride to his side, He will call us to Himself. No more shame, no more embarrassed admissions. Instead, chosen. Wanted. And renamed by our one true love.

> *In a very real sense not one of us is qualified, but it seems that God continually chooses the most unqualified to do his work, to bear his glory. If we are qualified, we tend to think that we have done the job ourselves. If we are forced to accept our evident lack of qualification, then there's no danger that we will confuse God's work with our own, or God's glory with our own.*
>
> —Madeleine L'Engle, *Walking on Water*

Day 28

Who Am I?

Find a quiet room or corner, take a seat, and close your eyes. Consider the names and labels you've lugged around for too long. What are they? Make a list, then tear it into a hundred pieces. Those names no longer apply. Ask God to replace these lingering labels with the names He calls you instead. Don't rush, don't leave your place of quiet too quickly. Let the God who loves you rename you.

Day 29

I Am Blessed

How much more will your Father in heaven give good gifts to those who ask him!

—Matthew 7:11

No one wants to spend Thanksgiving Day in the ICU. Especially not a girl who has long claimed it's her favorite holiday. But last year I did exactly that.

After a difficult, daylong surgery to remove two-thirds of my tongue and the cancer lurking inside, doctors sent me to the intensive care unit to guard against further complications. I appreciated their attention to detail, valued their concern. But spending Thanksgiving in the hospital wasn't my idea of a festive holiday celebration.

While the rest of America carved up turkeys and served up thick slices of pie, I lay in a hospital room enjoying a delicious IV drip. I wasn't allowed to eat or drink, not even ice chips. Instead, I listened to the sounds of nurses celebrating the holiday from their station. I smelled hints of a holiday meal being whipped up in the hospital cafeteria. Even with my door closed, I couldn't escape the constant reminders of all I was missing.

It's hard for a girl not to feel sorry for herself when faced with such a day. I remember looking out my window at the quiet Denver streets, imagining the memories being made inside so many cozy homes. With each beep of my many lifesaving devices, with each twinge of hunger in my stomach, I felt farther and farther away from the holiday.

Thanksgiving is about gratitude for God's blessings, for good food, sweet relationships, and laughter. Alone in a hospital room, I enjoyed none of the above.

Captive to my circumstances, I wrestled with questions I couldn't resolve. *What if I'd never gotten sick? What if the doctors had followed a different plan? What if . . . What if . . . What if?* Those were the questions on which I feasted that Thanksgiving Day. And with each question, I felt more and more sick. Like bars of a cell, the what-if's penned me in, interfering with my ability to practice gratitude.

At times I wonder how Paul—once named Saul—managed to live without the what-if's. In all of his New Testament writings, I don't hear him pining away about what might've been. I don't read any self-loathing for his years of misdirected zeal. I don't see him griping about his hardships or whining about his pain. I'm sure he had his hard moments. He was human, after all, and had plenty of reasons to play the victim. Still, he didn't look at his life as a series of unfortunate events.

"I count all things to be loss in view of the surpassing value of knowing Christ Jesus my lord, for whom I have suffered the loss of all things, and count them but rubbish so that I may gain Christ, and may be found in Him" (Phil. 3:8–9 NASB).

You see, blessedness is more a matter of perspective than a change of circumstance. Paul understood this, after enduring far more pain and persecution than one person should have to endure. This makes his words in 2 Corinthians 4:16–18 both hard-earned and profound: "Therefore we do not lose heart. Though outwardly we are wasting away, yet inwardly we are being renewed day by day. For our light and momentary troubles are achieving for us an eternal glory that far outweighs them all. So we fix our eyes not on what is seen, but on what is unseen, since what is seen is temporary, but what is unseen is eternal."

Paul didn't catalog his losses, he counted his gains. And his greatest reason for thanksgiving—among many others—was the fact that Jesus had found him, a proud, sinful, self-righteous man. And in spite of his ugly history, God granted him a future glory.

It took me a couple of days to pull myself out of my hospital-induced self-pity. It's not my favorite Thanksgiving memory, but it's by far the most powerful one. It was a day when my earthly treasure was taken away. In its place I held nothing but Jesus. A Thanksgiving-worthy gift, indeed.

I still have days when I struggle to celebrate Thanksgiving. It's not always easy to fix my eyes on what I cannot see. But if the ugliness in my story leads me to the feet of Christ, then my legacy is a beautiful and blessed thing indeed. The story I long to change is the same story that brought me to an enduring knowledge of the God who rescued me. In releasing the vision of what could have been, I'm finally able to see what God has done. And continues to do.

In the letting go of losses, you and I finally see what we've gained.

We may lose the world, but we've gained the maker of it.

Pardon for sin and a peace that endureth,
Thine own dear presence to cheer and to guide;
Strength for today and bright hope for tomorrow,
Blessings all mine, with ten thousand beside!

"Great is Thy faithfulness!" "Great is Thy faithfulness!"
Morning by morning new mercies I see;
All I have needed Thy hand hath provided—
"Great is Thy faithfulness," Lord, unto me!

—Thomas Obediah Chisholm,
"Great Is Thy Faithfulness"

Day 29

Who Am I?

Most of us find it easy to focus on the temporal, immediate, and tangible. The huge project with a looming deadline. The teen who struggles. The diagnosis that threatens. The mortgage payment past due. It's understandable. The proximity and urgency of those things make them nearly impossible to ignore. However, Paul claimed that the secret of living blessed is developing eyes that see beyond the obvious. We are recipients of incomparable gifts, not the least of which is the fact that we've been chosen and loved by Jesus Himself. This is a blessing that can't be taken away even in a hospital room on Thanksgiving Day. Take a moment to catalogue your blessings. Although your life may be riddled with losses, ask God to give you eyes to see His great gifts.

Day 30

I Am His Heir

Do not be afraid, little flock, for your Father has been pleased to give you the kingdom.

—Luke 12:32

She gasped when she saw it sitting on the kitchen counter.

A tiara.

Not a real one. A cheap imitation from a craft store. I'd bought it as a prop for a speaking engagement. Knowing I'd likely never use it again, I'd searched for the cheapest one I could find.

My five-year-old couldn't have cared less, enamored as she was by its presence in her home. The prize of a princess. *On our kitchen counter.* For the love of all things Cinderella, she couldn't move.

"Mommy, what is that?" She pointed as she whispered.

Unpacking groceries and beginning dinner preparations, I explained my upcoming speaking engagement and told her how I planned to use it.

Unsatisfied, she said, "I think you should put it on."

Put it on? Why would I?

That's when I stopped my ever-frantic kitchen activity to see the wonder in my daughter's eyes. A tiara sat on our kitchen counter. A silver, sparkling, bejeweled tiara. The kind reserved for Cinderella and Sleeping Beauty and other princesses of uncommon loveliness. Who wouldn't want to wear it?

It didn't matter that the cheap material would tarnish in a month. To a five-year-old girl, royalty sat within reach. Have mercy, would a prince soon come riding through our door? Anything seemed possible.

This glimpse of her innocence softened my grown-up heart, just a bit. I'd long ago given up notions of fairytales and romance. Real life had weathered me beyond happily-ever-afters. But my girl's response interrupted my indifference.

She too knew about real life and the weathering that comes with it. She'd been born into a hard story, a fractured family mired in the chaos of addiction. In the first four years of her life, before she joined our family, she knew uncertainty, fear, and unpredictability. Enough to make any girl give up on fairytales.

Yet a spark of hope remained, in spite of life's best attempt to snuff it out.

And so I grabbed the tiara and put it on. You should've seen my girl smile. Me too. She knew something I'd forgotten: A tiara doesn't belong on a kitchen counter. It belongs on princess girl's head.

Just as a tiara is meant to be worn, we've been given a royal heritage that is ours for the taking. Paul says it this way: "The Spirit himself testifies with our spirit that we are God's children. Now if we are children, then we are heirs—heirs of God and co-heirs with Christ, if indeed we share in his sufferings in order that we may also share in his glory" (Rom. 8:16–17).

We are co-heirs of a kingdom! Jesus is God's firstborn, and we are His brothers and sisters. That means we've been promised royal position and given a crown.

For some of us, this promise of family is too farfetched. Real family proves far more dysfunctional than a dream. Broken marriages, betrayed relationships, abuse, and neglect galore. Like a bad movie that won't end, the family we never wanted manages to follow us in the brokenness we can't seem to shed. It's tough to be excited about an eternal family when we're up to our necks in an ugly earthly one. Thus we leave our crown on the kitchen counter or we carry it around like a cheap craft-store prop. We forget what it means, what it's worth. We can't believe something so good could be reserved for us.

But our immediate family is the prop, not the eternal one. Even those with a picture-perfect family enjoy only the barest hint of the glory that is yet to come. We have a real King with a real kingdom. And He's chosen you and me as sons and daughters. Heirs. With a secured place in the perfect family. No dysfunction or drama. Ever again.

You and I are passive recipients of powerful positions. Simply because of the will of a Father, the unfathomable grace of a compassionate King. Our inheritance is a matter of grace. We should receive it with the humility and gratitude warranted an undeserved gift. Even so, you and I can stand tall and proud in our unmerited position. It is knowing our unshakeable place in God's kingdom that gives us security in our earthly one.

That means you and I could learn a thing or two from my daughter. Although she has lost all hope of the restoration of her birth family, she hasn't lost hope for the wholeness of her eternal one. She's holding out for a happily-ever-after bigger than any fairytale she could imagine. Including a magnificent King and an impressive kingdom.

And one silver, sparkling, bejeweled tiara.

One of the tragedies of our life is that we keep forgetting who we are.

—Henri J. M. Nouwen, *Here and Now*

Day 30

Who Am I?

It's easy to allow our experiences with an imperfect family to influence how we think about our place in God's family. Take some time to consider how you might be letting your flawed heritage interfere with God's perfect promise. The former can leave you feeling bitter and filled with doubt. But knowing your place as God's heir provides a security nothing can shake. Ask God to heal you of the wounds of lesser families so that you can experience the full benefits of your place with Him.

Part 4

PRESENCE

Day 31

I Am Not Alone

I am with you and will watch over you wherever you go.
—*Genesis 28:15*

I normally describe our family as borderline crazy. (I might be understating it.)

Two parents. Two businesses. Eight children. One really old dog.

But surgery, chemo, and daily radiation treatments for Mama turned our normal version of crazy into crazy on crack. How does a family function when Mama is dog sick? Not well, I can tell you that.

To get through, I knew I needed something outside the realm of cancer to focus on each day. Ideally, I hoped to find a book of the Bible with exactly twenty-eight chapters, one for each of my twenty-eight days of radiation and chemo.

I didn't find one. I found four. The Gospel of John, plus First, Second, and Third John. A perfect twenty-eight. Thus John became my faithful companion during those dark days.

For those who don't know, cancer treatment is cumulative, especially treatment on the head and neck. Like adding a single brick to your load each day, I didn't feel the weight of what was happening until the second week. But by treatment day 11, the impact was undeniable. I grew exponentially sicker with each day. How would I make it to day 28?

That day, I got up at 5:45 a.m., per my new routine, to shower, dress, and dry my hair (something that became less and less necessary). Ready for the day, I headed downstairs and parked myself in my favorite reading chair for thirty minutes before I needed to leave.

That's when I read John 11. For treatment day 11.

The story of Lazarus. And Jesus' raising him from the dead.

Ironic, yes? If it hadn't been for my sleeping family, I would've laughed out loud.

I've always loved the story of Lazarus. It has a good ending, and I'm all about good endings. That day, though, I wasn't as intrigued by the ending as I was by Jesus' emotions. John said Jesus loved Mary, Martha, and Lazarus (v. 5). And yet when He heard Lazarus was deathly ill, He waited (v. 6). Then when He finally arrived at their home much too late, He was "deeply moved in spirit and troubled" (v. 33). Ultimately, He wept (v. 35).

Whoa. Jesus wept?

I used to think Jesus cried because Lazarus had died. They'd been friends, they loved each other. It only makes sense to shed a few tears.

And yet Jesus knew long before He arrived that Lazarus' "sickness will not end in death" (v. 4). He knew a grand finale would trump the grief.

Still, He cried. Why?

If Jesus knew Lazarus would live in the end, why did God with Us weep? I can't presume to know the mind of God, but I believe He wept over the wide swath of suffering on that hillside. And perhaps, Jesus wept over our one-day world still riddled with those who weep and keen without relief.

People like you and like me.

That's when I started to cry.

Do You see my suffering, God? Do You see how I ache for all this to go away? Do You hear my cries, feel my pain? DO YOU WEEP FOR ME? I need to know!

For a minute or two, I waited in my chair for heaven to deliver my answer. Giant teardrops from heaven would've sufficed.

A girl can hope.

Instead, silence.

Fifteen minutes later, I parked at the cancer center. With a glance at my phone, I noticed a text message from my friend Kathi: "God and I had a long chat about you this morning. He wants you to know He's got this. You don't need to stress or worry this morning. Today, He's got you."

Not exactly a sky-splitting memo from heaven, but I walked into treatment day 11 with a little more hope.

Little did I know the greater message that was yet to come.

When I sat down in the waiting room, I again pulled out my phone. It'd been a couple of days since I'd last checked my blog. I needed to see if any new comments had come in. One had:

> *Dear Michele,*
>
> *I am working in customer service emails and just received an automatic email reply from your server with reference to this blog. I decided to check it out. What you couldn't have known is that I had just been in the ladies' room at work, crying out to Jesus, asking Him why He has allowed what feels like such unending suffering in my life this past year. And I believe that being the customer service agent that received your automatic email and was led by His Holy Spirit to this blog was our Heavenly Father's answer to my restless heart. Thank you!*
>
> *Love,*
>
> *Nina*

Two months earlier, I'd set up an automatic reply to messages coming into my inbox, knowing it would be impossible to keep up with emails during the long, crazy months of treatment.

Day 31

The day before treatment day 11, I'd ordered flowers for my mama from a national company. As a result, the company sent an automatic receipt to my inbox. My server then sent the automatic reply back, which typically is forever lost in the black hole of internet nothingness.

Not this time.

This time, my automatic reply landed in the inbox of a customer service rep named Nina. A girl who, only moments before, had wept and asked God if He sees her suffering. A girl who needed to know she wasn't alone.

Sweet, sky-splitting teardrops from heaven.

Okay, God. I hear You. And? Thanks.

Does God see our suffering? A thousand times, *yes*.

If you're in a place of suffering, please know this: God sees, even when it doesn't feel like He does. He is deeply troubled by your pain. He counts and carries your tears, even as He sheds His own. He will not leave you alone.

In me there is darkness,
But with You there is light;
I am lonely, but You do not leave me;
I am feeble in heart, but with You there is help;
I am restless, but with You there is peace.
In me there is bitterness, but with You there is patience;
I do not understand Your ways,
But You know the way for me.

—Dietrich Bonhoeffer, *Letters and Papers from Prison*

Who Am I?

Admitting loneliness puts one in a vulnerable position, and yet most of us have experienced it at some point. What if we chose to look at our seasons of loneliness from a different perspective? It gives powerful evidence for how we've been created and who created us. This means loneliness needn't cause us embarrassment or shame. It can give us hope that the one who made us to need His presence plans to fulfill that need. Invite God to make you fully aware of His nearness. He has not left you alone. Ask Him to open your eyes such that the loneliness flies away.

Day 32

I Am

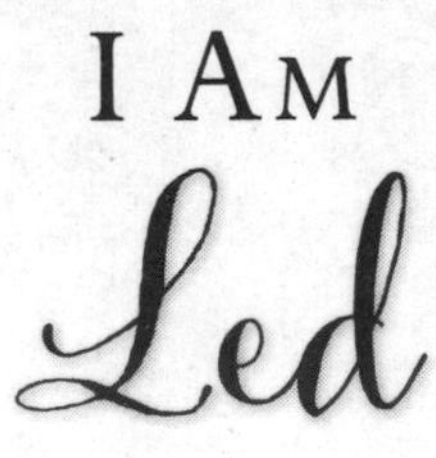

I am the Lord your God, who teaches you what is best for you, who directs you in the way you should go.

—Isaiah 48:17

The gift arrived without fanfare: a homemade T-shirt, a children's Bible, and a small card. On the T-shirt, handwritten in bright fabric paint, were the six letters of my seven-year-old daughter's name. On the card, handwritten in the script of her Sunday school teacher, was the Scripture reference Jeremiah 29:11. Then these simple words: "God has a plan for you!"

Without hesitation, my girl reached for her new Bible to discover the secret of Jeremiah 29:11. I helped her find book, chapter, and verse, and then together we read the words of the prophet Jeremiah.

"'For I know the plans I have for you,' declares the Lord, 'plans to prosper you and not to harm you, plans to give you hope and a future.'"

My little girl's face lit up with a smile like the sun. The God of the universe had great plans for her life! Even at seven years old, she relished the thought of His personal attention and care.

My daughter accepted the truth of Jeremiah's words without an ounce of skepticism. She believed it to be true as much as she believed the sun would shine.

It wasn't so easy for me. I still believed in God's goodness. I still believed in His love. But too many years of hardship had left me less than confident about His plans. Life hadn't turned out quite like I'd hoped. How was Jeremiah going to explain that?

And yet a look at my girl's face reminded me of the bigger story. Even at seven, she knew about life's knack for getting off course. By the time she was five, she'd lost one family and joined another—ours. And yet I did not doubt God's ability to bring good from the brokenness of her life. It was just a matter of time.

Thus the same was true for me. Isaiah's promise wasn't only for the lost and wandering people of his day. God included this reassurance in eternal canonical script so you and I, buried by our own lostness and wavering allegiance hundreds of years later, could know God's promised plan for us as well. A good plan. A plan that, although perhaps not exactly what we'd imagined, could not be more perfect for the overall story God's been writing from the beginning of time.

Sometimes life can feel a bit like walking through a minefield. Every day, we scan our circumstances, trying to make all the right decisions. We fear that one wrong move could cause the plan to unravel. So we tiptoe, cautious and afraid, agonizing over every move as if the future hinges on us.

- Should I buy a new house? Move to a new area?
- Is the guy I'm dating the one?
- Am I getting enough sleep? Too much sleep?
- Where should my kids go to school? Or should I homeschool?
- Which church is the right church for me?
- Am I being too hard on my children? Too soft?
- Should I quit my job, stay home, and focus on my family?
- Should I get another job so I can pay off my debt?

Day 32

The questions and unknowns twist and turn like an impossible maze. We do our best, no doubt about it. But the decisions and potential consequences never end, shaking us awake at night. If only God could overnight us a daily, detailed, step-by-step guide to knowing exactly what to do and when to do it.

Besides, where do we draw the line between submission to God's leadership and taking responsibility for our choices and actions? Personal responsibility is a noble quality. It's a good thing to make wise decisions and carefully weigh our steps. So how does this mesh with letting God lead?

Here's the deal: We don't have to have it all figured out. And we don't need to panic or worry or stay awake staring at the ceiling night after night. Why? Because the pressure is on Him, not you and me. As Jeremiah prayed, we can pray: "Lord, I know that people's lives are not their own; it is not for them to direct their steps" (Jer. 10:23).

If you and I determine to make our own way in this world to the absolute exclusion of God, then we have every reason to lose sleep. But if we keep our eyes focused on the one who holds the map and knows the way, if we ask for His leadership and search His Word for direction, we can trust He'll guide our steps.

For I know the plans I have for you, He says.

And His plans, even if different from our own, are always good.

O God, You Who are the truth, make me one with You in love everlasting. I am often wearied by the many things I hear and read, but in You is all that I long for. Let the learned be still, let all creatures be silent before You; do You alone speak to me.

—Thomas á Kempis, *The Imitation of Christ*

Who Am I?

We can count on the Holy Spirit to lead us through both the ordinary and extraordinary parts of our lives. Often, however, we're too busy directing our course to consider the counsel of God. Take a few moments to write down the biggest questions or decisions you're facing. Then block off fifteen minutes to take the unknowns to the one who knows the way you should go. Ask Him for clarity, focus, and wisdom for the way.

Day 33

I Am *Called*

But you, Israel, my servant, Jacob, whom I have chosen, you descendants of Abraham my friend, I took you from the ends of the earth, from its farthest corners I called you. I said, "You are my servant"; I have chosen you and have not rejected you.

—Isaiah 41:8–9

I imagine it was an ordinary day, not all that different from most of our days. Up before dawn. Stumble around getting dressed in the dark. Make a beeline for the programmable coffee pot.

Stop. Let's just take a moment to thank the Lord in heaven for programmable coffee pots. Yes, and amen.

So maybe Simon Peter didn't have a programmable coffee pot. But he must've grabbed something to eat and drink before he headed out the door for another long day of fishing.

That was his occupation. A fisherman. No college degree required. He'd likely learned the trade from his father, who had learned it from his father, and so on. It was hard, smelly work. But it paid the bills. And one can't be choosy when it comes to paying the bills.

I can't help but wonder if Simon ever dreamed of doing something more noble, more—how shall I say?—aromatic. But fishing was his calling.

Then an ordinary day turned extraordinary with the visit of a rabbi.

"As Jesus walked beside the Sea of Galilee, he saw Simon and his brother Andrew casting a net into the lake, for they were fishermen. 'Come, follow me,' Jesus said, 'and I will send you out to fish for people'" (Mark 1:16–17).

Come, follow me. No introductions or small talk, at least none Mark recorded. Instead, a radical invitation. To leave one calling for another. To abandon fish for people.

The Bible says Simon packed up and followed Jesus "at once" (v. 18). No hesitation or second thoughts. He heard the call and answered it. Period.

But I imagine his lack of doubts in that moment were multiplied in countless moments yet to come. Like when the religious leaders of the day mocked Jesus' unlikely choice of disciples. When naysayers questioned the sanity of a fisherman who claimed that Jesus was God. And by the way, great leaders are supposed to choose the wise and affluent, the strong and intelligent. Not a common fisherman, right? Yet Jesus called Simon anyway.

I know what it's like to have someone question my calling. Just hours before I wrote these words, I glanced at the online reviews for a podcast I'd recorded. I've recorded well over a hundred interviews and rarely read the reviews, but today I thought processing some feedback might help me improve.

Instead, I read a couple of harsh rebukes. Not constructive criticism, not even the honest feedback of someone who was less than a fan. Instead, individuals who questioned whether I have what it takes. Surrounding those verbal swords sat plenty of affirmations. But there's something nearly debilitating about a single person who questions your calling. It cuts at the core, especially when made public.

It's never fun to be on the receiving end of hurtful words. I may act tough, but the truth is criticism usually stirs up questions and self-doubts.

Especially now. Now that my speech is impaired and I struggle significantly to do what I love. Is a speaker who can't speak without tremendous effort still qualified to speak? Do my lack of articulation and clarity disqualify me from my calling? Honestly, some days I wonder.

And yet the calling wasn't mine. Just as Jesus stood on a beach and spoke to a fisherman, Jesus stands in front of us and speaks the same words: *Come, follow me.*

The calling has nothing to do with our qualifications. Jesus didn't choose me to be a messenger of truth because I was polished and professional. He chose me because He wanted to. And He's done the same for you. Jesus sees our willingness, and that is enough.

"But you are a chosen people, a royal priesthood, a holy nation, God's special possession, that you may declare the praises of him who called you out of darkness into his wonderful light" (1 Peter 2:9). Those are Peter's words, spoken years after Jesus called him out of a boat and onto a dusty road. Follow Jesus he did. He may have had moments of doubt, but they were soon overshadowed by the confidence that comes when you know your calling is from God.

A chosen people. A called people.

Peter. And you and me.

Criticism and questions are part of the path. But if we keep our eyes focused on the one who leads the way, the voices of naysayers will fade away.

As long as I dwell on my own qualities and traits and think about what I am suited for, I will never hear the call of God. But when God brings me into the right relationship with Himself, I will be in the same condition Isaiah was. Isaiah was so attuned to God, because of the great crisis he

had just endured, that the call of God penetrated his soul. The majority of us cannot hear anything but ourselves. And we cannot hear anything God says. But to be brought to the place where we can hear the call of God is to be profoundly changed.

—OSWALD CHAMBERS, *MY UTMOST FOR HIS HIGHEST*

Who Am I?

Although it's human to want the approval of others, we don't need it. Just as an ambassador is called to represent his country in a foreign land, God has called each one of us to represent Him by following Him. You may doubt your qualifications, but God guarantees He has given each of us gifts and talents to use for His purposes. And although counsel can help us hone our gifts, mean-spirited criticism—from within or without—merely distracts us from it. Today, ask God to confirm His call on your life. Invite Him to clearly mark the paths He'd have you take. And ask Him to buffer you against the unwarranted criticism of others and make you faithful to Him alone.

Day 34

I Am

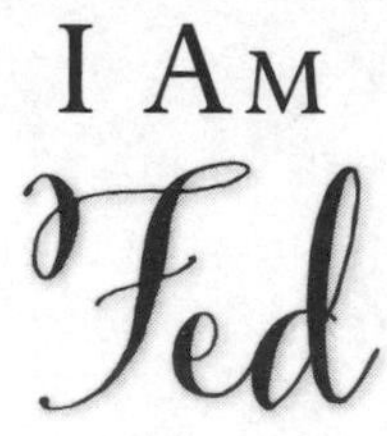

I will rain down bread from heaven for you.
—Exodus 16:4

I'm a hoarder.

Not in the sense of the reality television show, thank heavens. I can't watch that horror for even five minutes without developing hives.

No, you will not find piles of junk or garbage or trinkets clogging my house from floor to ceiling. I'm quite the opposite. A neat freak to the core. I like it that way.

But when it comes to food, I tend to stockpile. Perhaps it's because I'm a foodie at heart. Or maybe it has something to do with the fact that I am the primary chef for a large and chronically hungry family. That means planning and preparing meals takes up a large chunk of each day. Not to mention multiple two-shopping-cart trips to the grocery store.

Hellooooooo, second mortgage.

Or maybe my food hoarding has nothing to do with those things at all. Perhaps, at root, it's more about fear.

When it comes to food, I like the safety of stocking up. Not that I eat it; I simply need it nearby. Just in case. This urge to guard against hunger has only increased after multiple surgeries that compromised my ability to eat normally. I'm afraid of starving without the resources to be fed. Feeding tubes and no food by mouth for months at a time will do that to a girl.

My chronic hunger goes beyond food, however. There's a soul hunger I find myself equally compulsive to satisfy.

A hunger for approval from those I love.

A longing for meaningful relationships.

A need to know I'm doing a good job and pleasing those I most respect.

A desire for my life to count and to capture the attention of the Creator.

Although the cure for this hunger may not be as obvious as grocery store runs and cooking marathons, the fallout can be far more dangerous.

John 4 tells of a woman who understood starvation of the soul. A Samaritan with a sordid history, she met the Savior one day while drawing water from the community well. What began as a daily chore turned into a life-changing encounter.

"Will you give me a drink?" This was the first thing Jesus said to the woman (John 4:7).

She hesitated, confused by His crossing of gender and racial barriers by speaking to her. He was a Jew, she a Samaritan. Two cultures that mixed as well as oil and water. And yet He had spoken to her, had asked her for a drink. She questioned why: "You are a Jew and I am a Samaritan woman. How can you ask me for a drink?" (v. 9).

He responded in riddle, encouraging her to think beyond the physical well and physical water: "If you knew the gift of God and who it is that asks you for a drink, you would have asked him and he would have given you living water . . . Everyone who drinks this water will be thirsty again, but whoever drinks the water I give them will never thirst. Indeed, the water I give them will become in them a spring of water welling up to eternal life" (John 4:10, 13–14).

His riddle must have perplexed her as it perplexes me. Living water? Water that never needs to be replenished? Thirst that never comes back? That's quite a promise.

And yet promise it He did. According to John, the woman had had five husbands and was living with a man she wasn't married to. We don't know much about her story, but it's safe to assume she'd been "hoarding" relationships because her heart was desperate to be fed.

I don't have a history of five husbands, but I know what it's like to find my filling in lesser places. In my hunger of heart and soul, I've been known to compromise what is right and good to find a scrap of attention I desperately needed. The problem is the things I thought would satisfy made me even thirstier than before.

Have you ever been there? Do you know the desperation that can lead you to find satisfaction in a temporary well? And it's not always other people that pull us from the living water. At times it's money. Or food. Or success. Or awards. Or the next promotion. Or the drive to be perfect.

We've become experts at quenching our thirst with lesser loves. But like addicts who always need a bigger hit, we find nothing ever satisfies.

We need a different kind of well with a different kind of water.

And, thank the Lord in heaven, we have one. He offers to quench our every thirst and feed our hungry souls, day after day. He is not turned off by our need, nor annoyed by our regular walks to the well of His presence. He knows before we do exactly what our souls crave. And He promises to dish out a feast that can't possibly compare to any other fare.

If you don't feel strong desires for the manifestation of the glory of God, it is not because you have drunk deeply and are satisfied. It is because you have nibbled so long at the table of the world. Your soul is stuffed with small things, and there is no room for the great.

—John Piper, *A Hunger for God*

Who Am I?

Temporary wells can be quite tempting. Relationships. Food. Family time. Even community service and church ministry can become shallow substitutes for living water. These aren't bad things, unless they become the primary source of our filling. Then it's only a matter of time before we're disappointed by their inability to fully satisfy. Spend a few minutes in honest contemplation: Where do you typically walk to find your fill? What are your go-to wells? Only Jesus can cure every thirst, every hunger. Tell Him what you crave most, and ask Him to help you find your fill in Him. *Satisfy us with Your unfailing love!* (Ps. 90:14).

Day 35

I Am

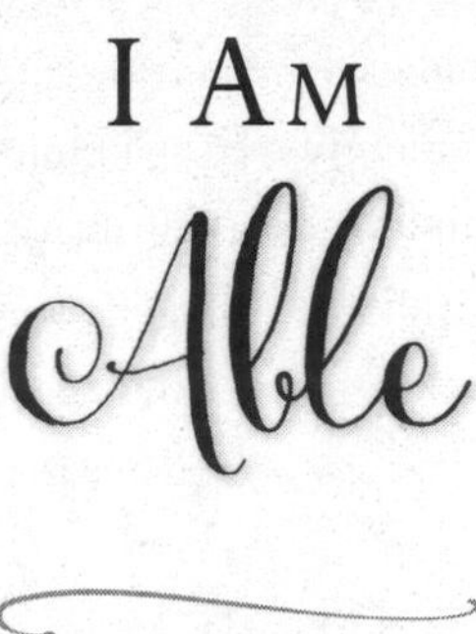

I am the vine; you are the branches. If you remain in me and I in you, you will bear much fruit; apart from me you can do nothing.

—John 15:5

In our back yard sits a beautiful cherry tree.

It's my favorite tree by far, boasting trunk and branches thick enough for my children to climb. Blanketed in lush green leaves, it provides both privacy and shade while my husband and I savor warm summer afternoons on the deck. Even better, every May our cherry tree blooms, offering up fragrant pink flowers as the first hints of a delicious cherry crop.

Until this May.

Everything appeared fine at first, the tree budding in earnest and promising to do what it's always done. But halfway through the budding process, the cherry tree simply stopped growing. The buds stalled in progress, appearing frozen in time. It was as if they didn't have the strength to finish their bloom.

It's now been months since May. The buds remain unopened. Spring never delivered blossoms and summer never delivered fruit. During a long, hot July, our leafless cherry tree offered no shade.

After doing a little research, I discovered ours is not the only tree that experienced such a fate. I'd assumed the cause had something to do with an unusually cold and wet spring culminating in a Mother's Day freeze. But that was merely the final knife blow. The death of our beloved cherry tree began long before that.

Months before, when fall was about to give way to winter, Colorado experienced a sudden and dramatic cold snap. Weeks before, we'd been given the gift of a warm, balmy fall. Turns out that wasn't so much of a gift for the trees. The warm temperatures did nothing to help the trees prepare for winter. Then in early November, the temperature dropped more than forty degrees in half a day and remained frigid for a week. Because they hadn't finished their winter-ready hardening process, the trees experienced a sort of flash-freeze. Arborists say the tender sap of fruit trees, in particular, struggled to recover, leaving tens of thousands of trees weak throughout the winter. Then, a tough spring and Mother's Day.[7]

It wasn't a single blow that brought my cherry tree down, but a thousand small "cuts."

I've spent a lot of time looking at that tree over the past several months. I'm hesitant to uproot it, hoping a lengthy rest might give it a chance to repair and once again grow. And as I wait for a rebirth, I find myself reflecting upon this often fragile life.

We're not all that different from my cherry tree. At times we can be lulled into a false sense of safety during a sweet, uneventful season. We stop making preparations for winter, stop thinking about the up-and-down nature of this unpredictable life. Instead, we pour ourselves fully into the laziness of balmy living, disregarding the reality of the change certain to come.

Then, almost overnight, the temperature drops. A blizzard catches us by surprise. A cold snap cracks our core.

Ill-prepared as we are, we grow weak. In shock, we stop growing, stop blooming and blossoming. Then, when one unexpected blow turns into two or three or four over the course of weeks or months or years, it's enough to take us down.

Just as the trees can do nothing to control the temperature, we can do little to strong-arm our circumstances. Winter can and will come, often when we least expect it. However, unlike my cherry tree, you and I have access to an unshakeable source of life: "Remain in me, as I also remain in you. No branch can bear fruit by itself; it must remain in the vine. Neither can you bear fruit unless you remain in me" (John 15:4).

Jesus' words of warning to us living, walking fruit trees.

Bad weather is bound to come. But we can prepare for it. And we don't have to endure it alone. If we want to have the muscle to make it, whatever may come tomorrow, we need to be invested with Him today.

Let's make a promise, shall we? Let's not be unprepared. Let's not allow warm weather to fool us into thinking winter will never come. You and I both know it's simply a matter of time. Instead, fully awake, let's make preparation. Let's soak up the Word and ask God to fortify us—heart, mind, and soul. Let's pray, pray, pray, inviting the sap of the Spirit to restore and establish us, "strong, firm and steadfast" (1 Peter 5:8).

His strength is our strength. We are able because He is able. And He offers us everything we need to thrive.

Quietude, which some men cannot abide because it reveals their inward poverty, is as a palace of cedar to the wise, for along its hallowed courts the King in his beauty deigns to walk.

—Charles Spurgeon, *Lectures to My Students, Volume 1*

Who Am I?

Describe your season of life. Is your soul bursting with new life like spring? Or does your heart feel a bit cold and dead like winter? Seasons come and go, and yet you and I can learn to thrive regardless of the temperature. Reconnect with your roots. Soak up God's wisdom and presence. Allow Him to show you what you're capable of—in season and out—with Him. And for those of you in a season of ease, celebrate it! But don't waste it. Just as the summer always gives way to fall, change will come. How prepared are you for winter?

Day 36

I Am Desired

For the Lord *has chosen Zion, he has desired it for his dwelling, saying, "This is my resting place for ever and ever; here I will sit enthroned, for I have desired it. I will bless her with abundant provisions; her poor I will satisfy with food. I will clothe her priests with salvation, and her faithful people will ever sing for joy."*

—*Psalm 132:13–16*

Seven years old and they'd never seen the ocean before.

Which is why, two years ago on a family vacation to California, we spent a full day at Huntington Beach with our littlest children.

With their first glance at the endless expanse of water, my little ones' eyes widened and they gasped in delight. It took two seconds for them to drop towels and shoes and sprint to the water's edge.

For two solid hours they giggled and squealed. Running into the surf, then running away, as if the ocean were a pouncing monster. With each venture into the salty water, they grew more courageous, more confident. They splashed and played and laughed until their purple lips and goosebump-covered legs couldn't take it anymore.

All this time, Mimi—my mom—took pictures. It was quite a sight, seeing these little ones taking in the ocean. We wanted to capture as much of it as we could.

Which was all well and good until I realized her camera was also aimed at me. A fortysomething woman splashing and laughing right along with the littles in her swimming suit.

Somebody save me.

At that moment of realization, I grabbed a towel with one hand and my mother's digital camera with the other. I scrolled through the files for incriminating evidence. I could not allow my I'm-not-sixteen-anymore body to be captured for all eternity on a JPG file.

Ugh. Not only did my dear mother capture picture after picture of my overly exposed self, nearly every pic was taken from behind and below, as she sat on the sand and pointed her Canon up toward us running in the surf.

Now, friends. We all know the proper way to take a photo. And this is not it.

The appropriate way to take a photo of a woman over the age of twenty is to lift the camera above the head and point down. Ten or twelve feet above, if possible. In that way, she can lift her chin (thus disposing of the baggage) and stretch her neck (again, the baggage). Not only will this angle produce a young and trim face, it will shrink the size of her hips significantly.

Trust me on this. You're welcome.

I reached for the delete button, sick at what I saw.

My first thought?

How could my husband possibly want a woman like me?

Fast-forward two years and subtract twenty-five pounds. After twenty-four-hour nausea from chemo and radiation, I'd wasted away to skin and bones. Clothes fell off me, skin sagged. A glance in the mirror revealed a gaunt shell of a woman. Pale skin, sunken eyes, swollen cheeks and lips. The body that used to run half-marathons and compete in triathlons showed zero tone and muscle. Everywhere—legs, arms, neck, stomach—scars marked where the surgeons had been.

My first thought?

How could my husband possibly want a woman like me?

Two years and twenty-five pounds separated the two me's. In neither case did I feel attractive or desirable. Which tells me something: desirability isn't about size or shape, even if we think it is.

Our culture draws a thick line of connection between appearance and desirability. Those of us who struggle with feeling less than attractive conclude we're not desirable or wanted. At the same time, there's nothing wrong with putting a little effort into our appearance. Call me vain, but I enjoy hair highlights and makeup. I like getting a pedicure and dressing in a new outfit. It makes me feel good.

But what about when life strips me bare? Is the unpowdered, unstyled, unpolished, undone me enough?

Psalm 132 talks about God's choosing of Zion—Jerusalem—as His home with His people. At that time, God's presence dwelt in the temple, in the Holy of Holies. This was sacred space to God's people, for they knew His nearness there.

Fast-forward a few thousand years. After Jesus' death, resurrection, and ascension to heaven, God sent the Holy Spirit, the gift of His presence dwelling in His people. No longer do we need to trek to a temple for His nearness. Now He dwells with us, in us.

Human desire is fickle and never satisfied. It's based on factors that can change from moment to moment, season to season.

Divine desire, however, is rooted in everlasting love. As a groom longs for his bride, God waits at the front of the room, anxious for the first glimpse of His beloved. He doesn't see size or shape, height or hair color. He sees love. Ironically, when we finally choose to see Him, rather than ourselves, in the mirror, we'll end up being far more beautiful than ever before.

My friends Becky Johnson and Rachel Randolph said it well in their book, *Nourished*: "There's nothing more beautiful, no more nourishing presence on earth, than a woman who lives loved, who knows her Father calls her Darlin' and loves to shower her with reminders of His tender caring."[8]

There's nothing more desirable than a woman who already knows she's desired by a Groom who can't wait to take her home.

Thou hast made us for thyself, O Lord, and our heart is restless until it finds its rest in thee.

—Saint Augustine, *Confessions*

Who Am I?

Although there are significant differences between human love and divine love, one gives powerful hint of the other. Think of your most beautiful experiences of human love and desire. Even your best memory is the barest representation of God's desire for you. He has pursued you and wooed you, from before your birth, in all your different shapes and sizes. Where human love ends, God's love remains, and He perfectly fulfills what human love lacks.

Day 37

I Am Carried

I have made you and I will carry you.

—Isaiah 46:4

By 6:30 a.m., my husband and I were up, dressed, and ready for the big day ahead.

It took a little more time to get four kids ready. Ranging in age from six to sixteen, they required attention and constant reminders. "Do you have your socks? Did you brush your teeth? Where are your tennis shoes?" All ordinary parts of every day. And yet they remained clueless about what to do.

Don't even get me started.

Once mom, dad, children, and grandparents had shoes tied and bags in hand, we locked up our hotel room and made our way out into the terrifying wilderness of greater Los Angeles. We told the kids we were running a few errands, that we had a few things to do before we continued our family vacation. The sixteen-year-old knew otherwise. He was far too savvy to fall victim to our secretive plans. But the little ones? They were none the wiser. They simply buckled into their car seats and settled in for the drive.

Thirty minutes later, their innocent faces took on an entirely different expression.

Surprise. And complete, head-to-toe joy.

Our so-called family errand had landed us right at the front gates of Disneyland.

Thus began our one-day family adventure at the Happiest Place on Earth. It was our little ones' first Disneyland experience. Our trip allowed us only one day there, so we determined to make the most of it. Up before dawn, at the park when it opened, and ready to play until the stars appeared at night.

And boy did we play! We rode nearly every ride, collected character autographs, ingested far too much food, and probably walked fifteen miles. Which is why the Cushatt Disneyland Extravaganza nearly required wheelchairs for the grownups by the time the sun had set.

We were exhausted, utterly and completely. My feet hurt. My head hurt. My stomach hurt. Did I mention all the food? We didn't want to miss the closing day parade and the opportunity to squeeze in a couple more rides. But I wasn't sure my feet could take a single additional step.

And then my six-year-old girl tugged my shirt and looked at me with her best puppy-dog eyes: "I'm tired, Mommy. Will you carry me?"

At this point, I could barely carry my own head. I swear it grew by twenty pounds somewhere in between Splash Mountain and the swirling magic tea cups. Carrying a sticky, sweaty forty-pound six-year old did not land on my list of fun things to do.

And yet I couldn't ignore her weary eyes. For perhaps the first time in her life, she'd expended every ounce of her seemingly limitless energy, dancing through Disneyland like a human version of Pooh's Tigger.

But she'd hit her limit. One look at her face and I knew she'd sleep like the dead that night. Me too. Even so. I lifted her little self into my arms, allowed her to drape her arms around my neck, and nestled her face and chin into the hollow of my neck.

When I felt the warm exhalation of her breath on my skin, I momentarily ached for a return to childhood, when I could trust arms bigger than mine to carry me when life grew too hard to endure. Is there anything more reassuring than the knowledge that there is someone bigger and stronger able to lift us above the struggle? Even so, a day came when I realized that my parents, in spite of their strength, were not above life's difficulty. As they aged, they grew weak. And as I matured, I saw them as they were: human, flawed, and, at times, tired. Full of love and devotion, but unable to carry me.

Life is far from the fantasy of Disneyland. Although I've been blessed with seasons peppered with hints of happily ever after, the difficulty and pain and grief of this life still show up. And these realities can wear me down and make me far too tired to go on.

That's when I discover God's promise to carry us isn't empty.

I've lost track of how many dark nights He's carried me through. Tough high school years. A painful miscarriage. An unexpected divorce. Single motherhood. Adolescent motherhood. Blended family. Financial insecurity. Spiritual uncertainty. Illness and disability. And each time I grew too tired to walk, I looked up and cried to my Father, *I can't do this, I have nothing left. Please, God. Carry me?*

He did. Without hesitation, without condition. No complaints about His weariness. No sighs of exasperation or rolling of His divine eyes.

Instead, His sure arms wrapped around me, my face nestled in His neck.

What is weighing you down right now? What feels far too heavy for your weary arms to carry? The weight of it all needn't rest on your shoulders, you know. He is with you. And He will carry you.

"Come to me, all you who are weary and burdened, and I will give you rest," Jesus said (Matt. 11:28).

Yes, that. Always.

Why did Jesus still have wounds on His risen body? The traditional answer is that the wounds proved it was really he and not an imposter . . . But I believe the wounds had a deeper meaning with radically transforming implications that affect us through the ages. I believe the wounds were the sure sign that the eternal God through Jesus has never and will never ignore, negate, minimize, or transcend the significance of human woundedness. The risen Jesus is not so swallowed up in glory that he is beyond our reach, beyond our cries. He is among us, carrying wounds, even in a body of light. His every word and act shining forth the meaning and heart of God means that God's heart carries our wounds. He suffers with us.

—Flora Slosson Wuellner, *Feed My Shepherds*

Who Am I?

Are you tired? Does the world weigh you down, and do your circumstances overwhelm? You don't have to rely on your own strength. You don't have to roll up your sleeves and gut it out alone. You can ask the God who made you to carry you, as many times as you need. Make a list of those things you can't carry anymore, the challenges and worries and struggles that have worn you down. Give each a name. Then, lift up your hands and ask your Father to carry you.

Day 38

I Am *Needy*

Be careful not to practice your righteousness in front of others to be seen by them. If you do, you will have no reward from your Father in heaven.

—*Matthew 6:1*

I'd been awake since 3:30 a.m. Couldn't sleep for all the excitement. Or was it anxiety? Sometimes it's hard to tell the difference.

It was a big day. After months of anticipation and preparation, I launched a new online study of my first book, a five-week conversation about how to make peace with an unexpected life. It was a worthy project with potential to spark connection and life change. I knew this. And I was thrilled about what God might do.

But I also felt terrified. What if no one signed up? What if the content turned out to be terrible? What if I said something dumb or insensitive or did something foolish in front of all those people? What if, in the end, I came up short?

I checked my email no less than a dozen times that morning. I stalked

Facebook approximately every 43.9 seconds. Aaaaaaand I might've carried my phone around in my palm for hours.

I hate to admit it, but I acted a bit needy.

Now, let's not make T-shirts out of the title. For the love of my ever-dwindling self-esteem, my neediness needn't be broadcast any more than it already is.

It helps to know I'm not the only one. During one of my many online excursions that morning I noticed dozens of other men, women, and teenagers working hard to solicit affirmation. Countless bathroom mirror selfies and posts about personal achievements. Uncomfortable disclosures about private relationships. Self-righteous sermons about controversial topics. Long-winded descriptions of personal demons.

I'm all for authenticity and relationship. But honestly. Have we ever had a more self-consumed society? I don't think so, as evidenced by the massive growth of social media platforms. Whether it's inappropriate SnapChat videos or indiscriminate Facebook posts, our neediness is obvious. We're desperate for someone to see us. Even if it means we compromise our self-respect in the process.

Now, lest you protest, let's clear one thing up. To be needy is simply to be in need. To have a requirement for living that is yet unfilled. That makes every one of us needy to some extent. Because hours after breakfast, we'll need to eat and drink again. As humans, we're made with needs that must be fulfilled to sustain life. And not just food, clothing, and shelter.

We're made to need love. Acceptance. Purpose. And a place in community. That means our neediness is not unique to our generation. But now we expose it for all to see in wide-screen, HD clarity, God help us. Still not convinced? Spend fifteen minutes on YouTube or watching an episode of reality TV. We are a desperate people. And in our desperation, we've become broadcasters of our neediness.

Jesus didn't have much use for false fronts. Whether watching religious leaders flaunting their false righteousness or wannabe disciples manipulating for attention, He knew the depth of need lurking beneath all of the drama.

It's not that He didn't have compassion for our humanity. I think He made it very clear otherwise. He just knew we'd never be satisfied with human responses to our desperate demands. When you and I pretend to be someone other than who we really are in an attempt to garner more affirmations and accolades, we're doomed to disappointment. Because eventually our truest selves will show themselves plain. And human love will prove to be the less than perfect gift that it is. As long as we keep trying to meet our deepest needs in the shallowest pools, we'll keep bumping our heads on the bottom. Not only will our desperation become painfully obvious to everyone around us, but we'll wear out the world in our attempts to find our fill.

Only one person sees the true extent of our neediness and isn't the least bit put off by it. Only He can fill our vacuous souls with what we truly crave, once and for all:

- "Then your Father, who sees what is done in secret, will reward you" (Matt. 6:4).
- "Then your Father, who sees what is done in secret, will reward you" (Matt. 6:6).
- "And your Father, who sees what is done in secret, will reward you" (Matt. 6:18).

Only God knows how to turn a needy heart into a satisfied one. Rather than repeatedly jumping in the puddles of shallow affirmations, let's dive deep into the heart of the Father's affection. Those who are needy never leave His presence empty. Admit your need to the Father. Fifteen minutes with Him will fill you more and for longer than fifteen minutes anywhere else.

I Am Needy

Far from being a sign of weakness, only surrender to something or someone bigger than us is sufficiently strong to free us from the prison of our egocentricity. Only surrender is powerful enough to overcome our isolation and alienation.

—David G. Benner, *Surrender to Love*

Who Am I?

Admitting neediness is embarrassing. We're supposed to talk about how great we are, how strong we are, how un-needy we are. I believe, however, the admission of our neediness is the first step toward a permanent and lasting security. The truth is you and I are needy. But our neediness is, at root, simply the design of a Creator to keep us connected to Him. We are made for something far more than what this life has to offer. Today, rather than broadcast your neediness to an indifferent world or attempt to hide it behind a false front of strength, bring your honest, needy heart before a God who loves you and has everything you need to be whole.

Day 39

I Am

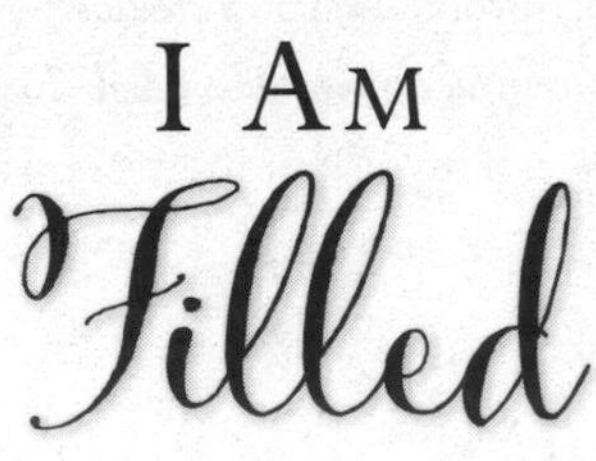

Blessed are those who hunger and thirst for righteousness,
for they will be filled.

—Matthew 5:6

I filled the raft with air, planning a quiet afternoon of lounging in the pool.

There's nothing so sweet as the slow days of summer.

Except, of course, when you have a houseful of bored children. And then the slow days of summer become a constant tension between planning activities together and praying—please, dear God in heaven!—that the first day of the new school year will soon arrive.

So maybe I'm not up for Mother of the Year. Almost overnight, I go from counting down the final days of the school year to counting down the days until school finally begins again in the fall. The never-ending glory and guilt of motherhood.

That day, exhausted from our new summer routine, I put my three littlest children down for a short afternoon nap. Then, wooed by the silence, I climbed into the pool. Just myself, a single blue raft, and sixty minutes of silent solar bliss.

Within minutes of relaxing in the sun, though, I started to sink. I felt the cold water climbing up my arms and legs, soon covering my waist and making its way toward my chest.

So much for my failproof flotation device. The raft had a leak and already needed a refilling. I could try to fix it. But that could take a half hour or more, a big slice of my sixty minutes. Instead, I blew the raft up one more time and climbed on.

Ahhhhhhhh.

Five minutes later, the water started to creepy-crawl back up my chilled body. For the next forty-five minutes, I climbed in and out of the pool, alternately blowing up the raft and attempting to lounge. Finally, I gave up.

So much for uninterrupted solar bliss.

Allow me to be blunt here. Sometimes I feel like a leaky raft. In spite of my regular attempts at solitude and self-care, I always seem in need of refilling. I seek more affection from my husband. More affirmation from my friends. More encouragement from my children. They try, honestly they do. But within moments of their filling, I feel myself leaking.

And I wonder, Is the problem with their efforts or with my raft?

More often than not, I blame my emptiness on them.

- "If only you'd tell me I'm beautiful and take me out more often," I cry to my husband.
- "If only you appreciated all the things I do for you every single day," I complain to my kids.
- "If only you understood my circumstances, my point of view, or made time for me," I whine to my friends.

Sound familiar?

Here's the million-dollar question (brace yourself; it's not an easy one): What, exactly, do we want when we feel we've gone empty?

In my more honest moments, I'd say I crave comfort. And peace. And an absence of tension and conflict. I want a life that goes according to plan, without any surprises. I want my children to make good decisions. I want my husband to meet all my needs. I want to eat chocolate donuts and drink lattes without gaining a single pound. Because *hello*—chocolate donuts and lattes.

In addition to comfort, did I mention I also want control? And calm. And finances that never run out. And food that magically appears on the dinner table.

"Blessed are those who hunger and thirst for righteousness, for they will be filled" (Matt. 5:6).

Jesus' words interrupt my whiny list of wants. Righteousness? Hungering for chocolate donuts sounds easier. Hungering for righteousness sounds like hard work.

Besides, what exactly does it mean to "hunger and thirst for righteousness"? I like the promise of being filled, but I'm not so sure about the how-to.

Simply, righteousness means to be right with God, to be justified. Not a bad thing. Problem is the Bible says I can do nothing to make that happen. Like trying to keep a leaky raft filled, there is no amount of effort I can expend to justify myself before a holy God. That's why God sent Jesus to become our righteousness. His death paid our price, patched our holes, allowing the righteousness of God to cover and fill. That means, in Christ, you and I stand whole before God, even while we're still very wrong.

Blessed are those who hunger and thirst for righteousness.

Righteousness is a tough concept to wrap a mind around. I confess I don't always grasp its requirements or my inability to meet them. Jesus' substitutionary gift on my behalf is beyond my ability to grasp.

And yet the price has been paid, the gift given, even when you and I don't always understand it.

I want nothing more than to want Him. To open my hungry self to His filling, knowing that only in Christ can my heart be full.

No more leaky raft, no more whining to husband and children and friends, "Fill me!"

Instead, wholeness before Holiness.

Filled.

There is no sweeter manner of living in the world than in continuous communion with God.

—Brother Lawrence, *The Practice of the Presence of God*

Who Am I?

About the time we think we've got it together, something happens to poke a hole in our strength. What would it feel like to be full, once and for all? Jesus said the secret to our filling lies in our longing for the right thing. We can hunger for more friends, a better job, a happier marriage. But sooner or later, the satisfaction will leak out. Instead, hunger for the covering of God in your life. Hunger for His glory and righteousness to be displayed in how you live. What would this kind of soul-filling make possible for you?

Day 40

I Am Provided For

Look at the birds of the air; they do not sow or reap or store away in barns, and yet your heavenly Father feeds them. Are you not much more valuable than they?

—*Matthew 6:26*

I will provide for them a land renowned for its crops, and they will no longer be victims of famine in the land or bear the scorn of the nations.

—*Ezekiel 34:29*

It's a terrifying thing not to know whether you'll get another paycheck. I've experienced this only twice in my adult life, thank heavens. Twice is more than enough.

The first time? When I suddenly found myself a young single mom of a one-and-a-half-year-old boy. Six days before Christmas, I moved from stay-at-home mom to single mom, with a car payment and a house payment due in less than two weeks. Where exactly would I get the money to pay those bills, not to mention for food, utilities, and everything else? Merry Christmas to us.

By February, I'd found a full-time job, secured child care, and begun the never-ending cycle of trying to stay on top of never-ending expenses. Cell phone? Cable television? New shoes or clothes? Not a chance. Splurges I couldn't afford. Even trips to the grocery store turned into a maze of tough decisions. Fresh fruit, vegetables, and meat were often crossed off the list, replaced by less expensive options like beans, pasta, and applesauce.

For two years, I worked long, hard hours and scrimped. Every month I wondered whether I'd make it, causing a chronic state of anxiety. If the unexpected happened, I had few if any resources to tap.

Somehow, we made it. To tell you the truth, I never quite figured out how the numbers added up. I knew my income as well as the nonnegotiable expenses. Each month the latter proved far more than the former. And yet somehow we always had enough. My son never went without clothes, food, and a place to call home. My used Toyota Camry held up without needing any significant repairs. Even more astounding, I came out of those lean years with zero debt, aside from my mortgage and car payment, and my bank account boasted a small savings.

I'd love to tell you this miracle was a result of my mad budgeting skills. But I know better.

The second season of financial unpredictability came several years into my second marriage. After nearly twenty years in the same career, my hardworking husband left his job to reach for a long-held dream: to start his own business.

I couldn't have been more thrilled or supportive. He had more than enough talent and know-how to make it work, not to mention the passion to fuel his dream. Still, we both knew the risk. We were about to walk away from a regular paycheck and dive into an unpredictable endeavor. What if we couldn't make it work? What if we couldn't round up enough business to keep our family going? What if our best efforts weren't enough?

It's now been thirteen years since my husband started his business.

It has surpassed our wildest dreams of success. Yes, we walked through some lean years and more than a moment or two of uncertainty. Once again, there were months when the numbers just didn't add up. We could pat ourselves on the back and assume our survival had something to do with our amazing entrepreneurial skills.

But we both know better.

In my first season of financial insecurity, the cause of the crisis sat outside myself. It wasn't something I chose. The second season was a choice. In both cases, however, I ended up with what I needed, when I needed it. No more. No less.

I learned something during those two seasons of financial famine. It's both simple and solid: God can be trusted to provide.

He can be trusted to see our needs and do something about them. What concerns us concerns Him, and He will provide what we need in ways we often don't expect.

This comes in handy when my need for provision extends beyond the financial. When my needs include peace, forgiving love, patience with my family, and wisdom for a complicated relationship.

And yet, to my great relief, God reaches deep to meet those needs as well, providing the wisdom or will or truth to soothe my anxiety. Just as He delivered daily manna to a group of wandering Israelites, God promises to dish up what we need. Rarely enough for tomorrow, but always enough for today.

No, the numbers don't add up.

But it's never been about the math. It's always been about the Provider.

Patience asks us to live the moment to the fullest, to be completely present to the moment, to taste the here and now, to be where we are. When we are impatient, we try to get away from where we are. We behave as if the

real thing will happen tomorrow, later, and somewhere else. Be patient and trust that the treasure you are looking for is hidden in the ground on which you stand.

—Henri J.M. Nouwen, *Bread for the Journey*

Who Am I?

Out of all creation—the fish, plants, trees, frogs, insects, elephants, and sparrows—only humans struggle with a chronic and debilitating case of anxiety. We are the pinnacle of God's creation, the culmination of His creative efforts. And yet we, alone, struggle to trust His provision. We could learn a thing or two from the creatures of the land and sea and sky. What do you need most right now? Financial provision? Comfort? Renewed relationships? Consider how the creatures of the earth trust their Creator's provision. Ask God to reassure you of His care and build up your trust. He knows your needs even before you do.

Part 5

RESCUE

Day 41

I Am Broken

He has sent me to bind up the brokenhearted.
—*Isaiah 61:1*

His name was John. That much I remember without any effort, although close to twenty years have now passed. So much of memory remains captive to the fog of time. But John is someone I'll never forget.

He sat across from my husband and me, both of us still in our twenties, new parents of a baby boy, and struggling. We'd driven the two hours to his ranch because he was a counselor. And he said he could help.

If anyone needed help, we did.

The details are private and painful, even these two decades later. But I can tell you this: in the short years of our marriage, I'd shrunk to a fraction of myself. Pain—unrelenting pain—does that to a person. Mine was a pain of the heart, of spending years praying for a marriage that could not be saved.

By the time I sat in front of John, I had no hope left. None. Years of effort had produced nothing but disappointment. I wielded anger like a shield, hiding my woundedness behind my hardness of heart.

John, bless him, did not pull away. He did not shrink from my searing cynicism, nor did he judge. Instead, he saw through the anger to the broken woman beneath. He pulled out his Bible and unfolded for me the words of Isaiah 61:

Day 41

The Spirit of the Sovereign Lord *is on me,*
because the Lord *has anointed me*
to proclaim good news to the poor.
He has sent me to bind up the brokenhearted,
to proclaim freedom for the captives
and release from darkness for the prisoners . . .
to bestow on them a crown of beauty
instead of ashes,
the oil of joy
instead of mourning,
and a garment of praise
instead of a spirit of despair.
They will be called oaks of righteousness,
a planting of the Lord
for the display of his splendor.

—VERSES 1–3

I'll never forget John's reading me those words. Beauty from ashes? Joy instead of mourning? I couldn't fathom it. My pain ran too deep.

John wasn't finished with me.

"God is not finished with you yet, Michele," he told me. "Someday you will be an oak of righteousness, a planting of the Lord for the display of His splendor. I know you can't believe it right now, but I believe it enough for the both of us."

John was right about two things that day.

One, I couldn't believe it. Not that day. It seemed too good to be true, another dream that would disappear the moment I reached for it. So I didn't reach for it. I couldn't afford to.

As it turns out, it didn't matter. Because John was right about one more thing: God did bind up my broken heart. He brought beauty from ashes, joy from mourning, praise from despair. It took time. *Years.* It took the hard work of healing, the help of a counselor, and intense seasons spent in the Bible, wrestling with my faith.

But somehow, as only the Sovereign Lord can do, God took this crushed woman and built her into an oak. Not a tower of perfection but a solid display of His ability to redeem even the most broken of people.

The Bible is full of examples of God's ability to grow oaks of His righteousness from broken individuals:

- Rahab the prostitute, who showed great courage when she hid the Israelites in her home and believed in the purposes of their God.
- Ruth the young widow from a pagan nation, to whom God provided a second husband, and whose son was included in the genealogy of the Messiah.
- Esther the uncle-raised orphan child, who eventually became queen and saved God's people from annihilation.
- Mary of Magdala, whose spirit once hid seven demons but was so radically changed by meeting Jesus that she followed Him even to His death and beyond.

Just as God bandaged and healed the lives of these women, God can bandage and heal our lives too. Regardless of the source of brokenness, He's more than able to bring forth new life. I know it feels scary to risk hope. It would be easier to hide behind a shield of bitterness or isolation. Or maybe mask the fear with a smile and the appearance of near perfection. Allowing ourselves to believe again could crush us beyond repair.

If your hope is placed in a spouse or a friend or a job or a bank account or even yourself, that's a real possibility.

But if your last scrap of hope is placed in the one with the power to bind up the broken, you will never be disappointed.

"He has anointed me to proclaim good news to the poor," Jesus said (Luke 4:18).

Yes, you are broken, He says.

Day 41

But your brokenness does not frighten Me. I will not shrink back. Because I've come for that very reason.

For you.

Be reassured: Where you are fragile, He can make you strong. Where you are wounded, He can make you whole. Entrust your pieces to His perfect hands, and watch His healing work begin. One day, you'll wake up to discover—joy!—He's turned your broken heart into Isaiah's oak, a planting of the Lord for the display of His splendor.

He did it for me. And He'll do it for you.

> *God does not ask you to give the perfect surrender in your strength, nor by the power of your will; God is willing to work in you. . . . And that is what we should seek for—to go on our faces before God, until our hearts learn to believe that the everlasting God Himself will come in to turn out what is wrong, to conquer what is evil, and to work what is well-pleasing in His blessed sight. God Himself will work it in you.*
>
> —Andrew Murray, *Absolute Surrender*

Who Am I?

It is no accident that Jesus chose, as His first official sermon, in a Nazareth synagogue, the words of Isaiah 61. On the inauguration day of His ministry, Jesus chose to connect with those of us caught in brokenness, captivity, and darkness. Don't skip over this too quickly, because His words carry significant implications for your value. Jesus could've called out the accomplished and devout and righteous. Instead, He reached for the broken. What does this mean to you?

Day 42

I Am

For I am the Lord, *who heals you.*

—Exodus 15:26

It was an emotionally charged moment, to be sure. For both the speaker and the audience. Everyone leaned forward, toward the face and the voice of the woman delivering her story, including me. Waiting—hoping—for a happy ending to the gripping narrative.

Moments before, she'd shared the story of a close friend who had been diagnosed with cancer, advanced and aggressive. From her place on the stage, she told an auditorium of women about her friend's horrific journey through chemotherapy and radiation, her struggle to cling to life, to battle this disease as a wife and a mom of two young children. The physical suffering alone felt unbearable, not to mention the weight of carrying around a not-so-favorable prognosis.

Things didn't look good. So they prayed. Their friends, their church, their small group.

God, heal! Make her whole! Deliver a miracle!

The women in the audience, including me, hung on every word. And many of us tracked the details of her story especially well. Because we knew.

Day 42

We'd been there.

We'd heard the doctor's words. Ingested the news like trying to swallow a camel. And then braced ourselves and dove deep into a treatment regimen that drastically altered the lives we once knew and loved. Forever.

For all of us sitting in our comfortable chairs in the auditorium, the speaker's story carried the discomfort of reality. We knew it could happen to any one of us. Thus the reason we leaned in, waiting for the story's end, hoping for a happily-ever-after.

To our relief, that happy ending came. After a grueling journey, the speaker's friend recovered. It has been six years now, and against all odds, her friend remains alive and cancer free.

The audience erupted in applause.

God is good!

God hears our prayers!

God heals!

You could feel the relief in the room. A communal exhalation of fear, replaced by an inhalation of peace.

But for some of us, our relief lasted only for a moment. Because at the same time we were celebrating the woman's healing, we were also realizing we'd not yet received our own. For some in the audience, prayers for a child's wholeness had ended in a small casket. Others had watched a parent or a friend or a spouse walk away from a relationship. And still, for many others—women not all that different from me—the word *healed* remained elusive. Whether chronic or terminal, their sickness continued in spite of their prayers.

What are we then supposed to believe about the God who heals?

Like our speaker and many in the audience, I too have dropped to my knees in soul-pouring petition. *God, heal! Make me whole!* I've lost track of the number of my desperate prayers. When my marriage failed and divorce seemed inevitable. When being a mom nearly ripped me apart.

And yes, when a cancer diagnosis stole my innocence and forced me to face death.

God, heal!

And yet my first marriage dissolved, and I became a single mom at age twenty-seven.

Parenting proved complicated and didn't end up at all like I imagined.

And yes, cancer showed up three times.

My prayers are just as fervent and faith filled as those who receive their happy ending. So where's mine? Where's my healing?

Still, who's to say my prayers haven't been answered? Perhaps not in the way I dreamed or wished. Perhaps not with perfect happily-ever-afters and cancer-free proclamations. But God has wrought a healing that has transformed me just the same.

For perhaps the first time in my life, despite my unhealed body, I can say I'm whole.

Bruised and beaten, yes. Exhausted and weary, absolutely. But the broken desperation that defined much of my people-pleasing life no longer dominates my existence.

Instead, wholeness. Completeness. Even in my unhealed imperfection. Because I've discovered a God who, somehow, heals more than a body; He heals a soul.

A day will come for all of us when healing—physical healing—will not arrive. For some, it will happen at a ripe old age. For others, at twenty-four or sixty-eight or forty-one. It's not a matter of if but when.

But the God who heals remains just as sovereign and powerful and loving when the healing doesn't come. Perhaps more so. Because it is only then that we are able to experience healing as it was meant to be from the beginning: complete. And forever.

I'll be honest. I still struggle with this from time to time. I don't understand why some people receive earthly healing and others do not. But we can trust that the God who heals loves us, even when we don't understand Him. There, in the thick of our questions, we can ask Him to show us His heart and purposes, to help us to see beyond healing to wholeness, of ourselves and the world.

No more waiting for Hollywood happy endings and doctor's calls. No more fear keeping us awake at night.

Instead, sweet wholeness. Forever.

They say of some temporal suffering, "No future bliss can make up for it," not knowing that Heaven, once attained, will work backwards and turn even that agony into a glory.

—C. S. Lewis, *The Great Divorce*

Who Am I?

Healing—or the lack thereof—is an emotionally charged subject for those of us who have prayed for it and haven't received it, either for ourselves or a loved one. And yet we all know a day will come when healing of our physical bodies will be denied. Death is a reality none of us escapes. God's promise of healing must be far greater and more spectacular than simply a temporary restoration of these bodies. What healing are you holding out for? Don't stop praying for it, don't hesitate to keep asking God for a healed body or healed relationship. But don't be surprised if the healing He brings you is even better than what you asked for.

I Am *Forgiven*

I, even I, am he who blots out your transgressions, for my own sake, and remembers your sins no more.

—Isaiah 43:25

I didn't mean to do it.

Well, maybe I did, just a little bit.

He'd hurt me. And so I responded in an appropriate, mature, grown-up manner.

I ignored him. For most of two days.

The way I saw it, my husband had forgotten my birthday. Well, he didn't actually forget. He just didn't mention anything for half a day. And by early afternoon, I felt I'd waited long enough. I felt it my duty to point it out to him. Complete with four-year-old theatrics.

As I mentioned. Appropriate, mature, and grown-up.

In hindsight, once the emotion had dimmed, I knew he hadn't meant to hurt me. It was an oversight. He'd been busy juggling kids and work that morning so I could work. Besides, he's not much of a morning person. His brain works best after lunch. Perhaps if I'd given him a chance, been a bit more patient, he would've wished me a happy birthday after all. It might've turned out to be a quite delightful day.

Instead, I jumped the gun. Then let unforgiveness take root. Not super productive.

Fast-forward a little more than twelve months. The date had been on my calendar for weeks.

In-studio Radio Interview. With Jenny. 1:30 pm.

I'd highlighted it in red, made sure I'd blocked off the rest of the afternoon to allow drive time to Aurora, Colorado, and back. I was looking forward to it.

But then the day came and, along with it, unexpected drama. The morning carried all the everyday chaos of getting children dressed, fed, and to school on time. But it was complicated by a last-minute doctor's appointment and a mad dash across town. Not to mention the anxiety that seems to accompany any trip to a doctor's office.

By the time I'd returned home, I felt drained. I crawled into bed and collapsed for a beautiful, long nap.

When I woke up, I made my way to my office and checked my email. An email from Jenny landed in my inbox: "Just checking to see if you are coming in for interview today? I have 1:30 p.m. on my calendar."

Oh no! The interview!

I glanced at my clock. Well after 3:00 p.m.

I felt sick. I'd never missed an interview or a speaking engagement before. Not showing up was simply inexcusable. I hated myself.

Within minutes I'd returned her email with profuse apologies for my blunder. There was no excuse, other than my preoccupation with my circumstances. Not much of a valid excuse at all. I clicked send and waited for her reply. When it arrived, I cringed and read it through one eye, certain I'd get an appropriate lashing. I deserved her frustration and disappointment. Instead, this: "Oh, Michele. God gives us all grace . . . Please don't give the miss today another thought . . . I totally understand and God brought to mind that you might have something else going on in your world that was bigger."

With a few words, she absolved my wrong. I nearly cried with relief.

Two contrasting stories, only months apart. In one, I doled out forgiveness reluctantly, stingily, demanding that a price be paid. In the second, I received forgiveness lavishly, without condition, with an abundance of love. One left both parties licking wounds. The other left both parties marveling at grace.

Here's what I can't figure out: if I know the bliss of receiving forgiveness, why am I so stubborn about giving it?

I wish I could tell you I've learned my lesson. That the birthday incident was a one-time tango with unforgiveness. But I've done the dance more times than I can count. Afterward, I pound my head and promise never to be so foolish again.

Until the next week or month or year, when I end up tapping my foot to another tune and forget all about the consequences of my unforgiveness the week or month or year before.

You know what I'm talking about, don't you? One moment we quote verses on grace, and the next we circle up and launch a griping session. In the morning, we show up at a church service and sing songs about God's merciful patience, and yet by the afternoon, we nearly scream over the phone at the customer-service representative who won't right all their wrongs.

We're a mess.

My best intentions and tireless effort aren't enough. In spite of my repeated promises, I make the same mistakes again and again. "I'm sorry" seems trite right about now. Forty-some years of "I'll do better next time" no doubt wears thin. How long until God refuses my pleas for forgiveness?

> *The Lord is compassionate and gracious,*
> *slow to anger, abounding in love.*
> *He will not always accuse,*
> *nor will he harbor his anger forever;*

Day 43

he does not treat us as our sins deserve
or repay us according to our iniquities.
For as high as the heavens are above the earth,
so great is his love for those who fear him;
as far as the east is from the west,
so far has he removed our transgressions from us.
—Psalm 103:8–12

As high as the heavens are above the earth.

As far as the east is from the west.

How long until God tires of our pleas for forgiveness? Never. Not after one year or two years or ten years. Not after a hundred requests or a thousand I'm-sorry's.

Why? Because we're good people and deserve a second chance? Because He's good and can't bear to judge?

Yes, He's good. And yes, He takes no pleasure in judgment.

But the answer to the why of absolution sits in verse 8 of David's psalm: "The Lord is compassionate and gracious, slow to anger and abounding in love."

It's not about our character; it's about His.

It's His perfection that lands us in an ocean of grace. Not ours. This is good news for those of us who get frustrated with our repeated failures. Because as long as God's character remains unchanged, His forgiveness will not fail. "I the Lord do not change" (Mal. 3:6).

That's the beauty of it. When our character fails, His character does not. He never grows weary of our humble repentance or tires of our constant need for forgiveness. Instead, He pours His forgiveness out on the broken and contrite.

And He does this because He cannot be anything other than who He is.

A God of compassion. A God of forgiveness. And a God whose love stretches farther than the distance between the east and the west.

Our courteous Lord does not want his servants to despair because they fall often and grievously; for our falling does not hinder him in loving us.

—Julian of Norwich, *Showings*

Who Am I?

As long as we think our absolution depends on our efforts, we remain slaves to ourselves. But to live in forgiveness is to live in freedom. How fully do you admit your need for forgiveness? What most stands in your way? God's grace is an ocean, His love unfathomable. Regardless of your transgressions, you have nothing to fear, my friend. Forgiveness awaits.

Day 44

I Am Saved

For God did not send his Son into the world to condemn the world, but to save the world through him.

—John 3:17

My mom sent me the picture yesterday, God bless her. She pulled it from a folder of old photos labeled "1970–1975." Usually pictures from that era frighten me.

Not this time.

I smiled when I saw it. Then, tears.

My mom, my dad, my little brother, and me.

Easter Sunday, either 1974 or 1975. Back when Mom sewed her own dresses and Dad sported wide ties and killer polyester pants. Matching, of course.

My memories of childhood Easters are no longer crisp and clear. They've faded with time, just like the photograph. But I remember a few things like it was yesterday.

Sitting at the dark-brown laminated kitchen table, the smell of vinegar burning my nose while I dipped hardboiled eggs into large coffee mugs filled with dye.

How the pink and green dye stained my fingers, and how I wiped them clean underneath the table top when my mama wasn't looking.

Searching frantically for Easter eggs in the back yard of our Arizona home, trying to gather more than my snotty little brother did.

Posing for family pictures on the lawn after Sunday-morning church services. Dressed in our finest. Smiling. Holding hands.

As I look at the little girl in the picture, I can't help but think of how much life has changed in the many Easters since the photo was taken. I see her small hand enveloped by her daddy's big hand. It never occurred to her that someday he'd be gone.

Easter Sundays are no longer the same. In part because one member of our family is now absent. In part because life over the past several years has changed me.

Easter means far more than it did before. It's no longer about egg hunts and baskets filled with candy, although we still have plenty of both. It's not about sitting through well-produced church services or a big Sunday afternoon meal, although we certainly enjoy those with great satisfaction.

They say it is the hard things, the painful things, that shake us from the status quo such that we develop eyes to see the beauty of this one life. There, heaped in our losses, we are forced to dig deep to uncover meaning we'd before missed. Perhaps that is why Easter carries more significance than it did before.

Easter means I have a friend who understands long, lonely nights filled with questions. It's the most sacred part of the Easter story for me. A thirty-three-year-old Jesus grieving in a dark garden of Gethsemane. Facing death with tears. He asked His friends to stay close, to help Him stay strong. He couldn't sleep, but they couldn't even stay awake. Oh, how I understand! For all my lonely, sleepless nights, I'm reassured I am not alone. He keeps watch with me, as only one who understands can.

Easter means I have a cosufferer who knows the agony of physical pain. I've experienced far more pain than I ever imagined. At times, I thought it would kill me. Other times, I hoped it would. At the same time, I see incredible suffering around the world, much of which dwarfs my own. I know this, wrestle with it. My heart can hardly bear it. Easter takes me, crawling, to the one who endured a physical suffering so heinous, so inhumane, by choice. Even more profound? He did it for you, for me, so we'd know we're not alone.

Easter means I have a Savior who faced death so I would no longer need to fear it. It is not an easy thing to face your mortality. Forty-year-old mamas shouldn't have to think about death. When fear creeps up, tempting me to worry about tomorrow, I remember the one who left heaven to kick death in the teeth, once and for all. Yes, death is reality. But Easter means He went first. And Easter means He beat it. And my daddy? The one holding my hand? Easter means he lives too.

Easter means I have a Father who will never leave, who will hold my hand through whatever may come. Behind every twist and turn in the Easter story, behind the long night in the garden, the horrible trial and death conviction, behind the procession along the Via Dolorosa and the climb up Golgotha to the nails and the cross sits one powerful truth: I am saved.

I don't know what you believe. Perhaps Easter means family time, scavenger hunts, and chocolate-covered eggs. I enjoy those things too.

But after I've endured and overcome so many difficult days and lonely nights, Easter means something more real and urgent and beautiful than ever before.

I need more than fluffy bunnies and chocolate-dipped eggs.

I need a Savior.

One who lived and died and overcame so I could overcome too.

The day in between the death and the resurrection hurts the most. Because it is here you and I wait, fighting to believe that He will do as He promised. Do we trust Him? Do we take Him at His word? Do we bank our very breath on something—someone—many call a fairy tale?

Yes, we do. Even today while we hover in tense expectation of the story's resolution. Because to those who believe today, life comes tomorrow.

I need Christ, not something that resembles him.

—C. S. LEWIS, *A GRIEF OBSERVED*

Who Am I?

Easter may be months away, and yet there's great value in remembering the Easter story any time of the year. Consider reading John 19–20 today. What does it mean to you that Jesus has saved you from death? Those of you who have brushed up against mortality understand a bit of this shocking gift. God died so that, even in earthly death, we will still live. Ask your Savior to restore to you the wonder of His salvation such that your life will look far different because of it.

Day 45

I Am Clean

I will sprinkle clean water on you, and you will be clean . . .
I will give you a new heart and put a new spirit in you; I will
remove from you your heart of stone and give you a heart of flesh.
—Ezekiel 36:25–26

Four days of tent camping in the Wyoming wilderness is good for the soul. But it does nothing for personal hygiene.

By the time our family returned home from the trip, a thick layer of grime covered every square inch of our gear and bodies. I doubt the boys noticed, accustomed as they are to dirt and stench. I, on the other hand, was quite certain I'd become unrecognizable, both in sight and scent.

On the upside, we all smelled the same brand of horrible.

As soon as we unloaded and unpacked, I sprinted to the shower. I couldn't peel off my clothes fast enough. Within a minute I stood, eyes closed, under a downpour of steaming hot water, where I stayed for a half hour.

I couldn't imagine anything feeling better. Hot water coursing over every inch of my head and body, removing dirt, both seen and unseen. Grime falling off me and disappearing down the drain, leaving a fresh soapy scent behind. By the time I finished my shower, my pink flesh nearly sparkled.

Clean! I'm clean!

Of course, by the following morning, I needed another shower. And another the next morning. And every morning after that. My day-to-day dirt isn't nearly as noticeable as my camping dirt, thank heavens. But I need daily showers just the same. In spite of my best efforts, I can't avoid filth. I need help staying clean.

Perhaps this is why I marvel at God's promise to make me clean. I know my propensity to get dirty. I know quite well that today's shower won't eliminate my need for one tomorrow. Even a half hour of scrubbing with soap won't keep me from soon being in the same need. And yet God promises the kind of shower that eliminates my grime, once and for all.

> *"Come now, let us settle the matter,"*
> *says the* Lord*.*
> *"Though your sins are like scarlet,*
> *they shall be as white as snow;*
> *though they are red as crimson,*
> *they shall be like wool."*
>
> —Isaiah 1:18

White as snow.

God promises to make the filthy, clean. Once and for all. Without the need to scrub ourselves free of our grime. But believing this isn't my only struggle. There's another: believing—to my core—how desperately I need it.

By midmorning most days, I've already come face to face with my dirt. I mean, what else can ignite an impatient mama like the before-school routine? Fighting children, complaints about breakfast, drama over what to wear and how to style an eight-year-old's hair. It's enough to make my Dr. Jekyll shrink and my Mr. Hyde appear.

Day 45

Even so, I soothe myself with reminders of my good deeds. The muffins I baked, the laundry I folded, the dishes I put away, the lunches I made. I even organized a before-school prayer. *I'm not that bad after all, am I? So I have a little bit of dirt. It's not much compared with the next guy.*

How quickly I forget that it isn't the amount of filth but the mere presence of it that robs a person of her purity. I spend very little time thinking about my need for a cleansing because I'm busy justifying the dirt I still carry. But the effort to appear clean works about as well as slapping perfume over a stinking corpse. It doesn't mask the smell; it only complicates it.

There's no doubt that we have a God who has not only offered us the promise of a soul-shower but also has the means and heart to follow through on it. But before we can fully appreciate the gift, we must know fully how much we need it. Only when we're aware of our grime are we likely to accept the cleansing God offers.

David's prayer of honest admission is a beautiful example to follow:

Have mercy on me, O God,
according to your unfailing love;
according to your great compassion
blot out my transgressions.
Wash away all my iniquity
and cleanse me from my sin.
For I know my transgressions,
and my sin is always before me.
Against you, you only, have I sinned
and done what is evil in your sight;
so you are right in your verdict
and justified when you judge.
Surely I was sinful at birth,
sinful from the time my mother conceived me.
Yet you desired faithfulness even in the womb;
you taught me wisdom in that secret place.

I Am Clean

Cleanse me with hyssop, and I will be clean;
wash me, and I will be whiter than snow.
—Psalm 51:1–7

I confess, God help me, I'm unclean. Body and soul. As are you. Even our best efforts to do what is right and good come up short, time and again. And unless we see the filth, we cannot escape it.

But for love, God offers to make us clean. Whiter than snow. Step into His mercy. Surrender to the shower of His grace. Watch the grime fall off and glorious cleansing come.

Come, Thou Fount of every blessing,
Tune my heart to sing Thy grace;
Streams of mercy, never ceasing,
Call for songs of loudest praise.
—Robert Robinson, "Come, Thou Fount of Every Blessing"

Who Am I?

In Romans 7:18–21, Paul provides a clear picture of our human struggle against sin. We all fight the same battles, no matter how we work to deny it or hide it. In our honest admissions, however, we are free to appreciate, with great joy, God's gift of a clean heart. What corners of your heart remain unclean? Is there an unresolved conflict that's left you frustrated with the filth? Ask the God of grace to come and drench you with His cleansing mercy.

Day 46

I Am Comforted

I am he who comforts you.
—Isaiah 51:12

The second the bus stopped at the corner, my little girl climbed off and ran as fast as she could toward where I stood.

Something wasn't right. She was crying.

Immediately my mind jumped to worst-case scenarios. Did someone threaten her at school? Had she hurt herself seriously in gym class? Good heavens, did a teacher or one of her friends die?

Turns out her wound wasn't quite so dramatic. But it hurt just the same.

Someone had told her they didn't like her anymore. In typical grade-school fashion, the mood of the relationship had turned sour on the playground. As a result, my girl fell out of the other girl's affection.

There on the street corner, I held her close while she cried. I was glad she told me. But what made me most proud is what she said next: "When we get home, can we cuddle?"

For years I've been working with my girl to learn how to ask for what she needs. It's hard for her, tough girl that she is. Typically she either guts it out or reverts to theatrics. Instead, we've been discussing how to use words to communicate needs. No drama, no false front of strength. Just an honest admission of hurts and what she needs to help fix it.

That day, on the street corner, she did just that. She expressed her hurt. And then she asked for my comfort. I was thrilled to oblige.

If only I could learn to do the same.

Most days I'm glad to be an adult. I mean, really. Who wants to travel back to the days of diapers and pureed peas? Or how about those adolescent years when pimples threw a facial party and peers found a way to make me apologize for my existence in the world? And don't even get me started on playground drama, homework, and early bedtimes.

Wait. That last part? I could totally go back and do that again. Sleep rocks.

For the most part, I'm glad the struggle of youth is behind me. Being an adult certainly has its rewards. No pureed peas topping the list.

When I'm hurt or discouraged or afraid, however, my adult skin wears thin. When bills demand paying and parenting proves impossible. When marriage is hard, friendships struggle, and doctor's appointments fill a calendar.

Then I wish to travel back in time, when a girl's greatest fears could be soothed in a mama's arms. Held close, all was well. To a child, there's nothing greater than a parent's ability to comfort.

But comfort doesn't come so easily to us grownups. Where do you and I go when relationships wound and the injustice of life stings? Who waits for us on the corner when we can't stop crying?

We adults carry such responsibility, don't we? Such blunt knowledge of the unfairness and volatility of this life. Even if we avoid news and media, fear and pain still have a way of finding us. We can't escape them. Who do we turn to for comfort?

Ourselves, more often than not. We either erect a false front of strength or cave in to a pattern of complaining. But neither the pretending nor the pining brings much relief to our aching hearts.

Day 46

There's a better way. The Bible is rich with examples of men who voiced their needs and asked God for His comfort. Even better, the Bible nearly explodes with examples of God's corresponding tireless affection. At times He comforted those He loved *through* their circumstances, and other times He comforted them *in* their circumstances:

- To the leader Joshua, overwhelmed by his new task: "Do not be afraid; do not be discouraged" (Josh. 1:9).
- To the Israelites enslaved by ruthless Egyptians: "I am concerned about their suffering" (Ex. 3:7).
- To the widow who had lost her only son: "Don't cry" (Luke 7:13).
- To the adulteress caught in her shameful sin: "Neither do I condemn you" (John 8:11).
- To the blind man longing to see: "Receive your sight; your faith has healed you" (Luke 18:42).
- To the sisters who had lost their beloved brother, "Jesus wept" (John 11:35).
- To the disciples, who ached because their friend would be leaving them, Jesus said: "And surely I am with you always, to the very end of the age" (Matt. 28:20).

And to those of us who wade through the deep waters of this modern life, longing for a world we've heard about but have not yet seen, Jesus promises:

- "I am going there to prepare a place for you" (John 14:2).
- And "I am coming soon" (Rev. 3:11; 22:7, 12, 20).

Regardless of your pain—whether physical, emotional, or spiritual—you don't have to pretend to be strong, nor do you need to succumb to your tears. Shed your grown-up skin. Become a child in the presence of a comforting Father. Like so many throughout the Old and New

Testaments, don't be afraid to expose your need and ask God for comfort. Then, count on Him to deliver.

"The Lord is close to the brokenhearted and saves those who are crushed in spirit," the Bible says (Ps. 34:18). Nestle in, my friend. Comfort is coming.

Tell God all that is in your heart, as one unloads one's heart, its pleasures and its pain, to a dear friend. Tell Him your troubles, that He may comfort you; tell Him your joys, that He may sober them; tell Him your longings, that He may purify them; tell Him your dislikes, that He may help you to conquer them; talk to Him of your temptations, that He may shield you from them; show Him the wounds of your heart, that He may heal them.

—François de Salignac de la Mothe Fénelon, *Spiritual Letters*

Who Am I?

A person's experience with human comfort—or the lack thereof—can have a powerful impact on their trust in God's comfort. If the comfort of a parent was absent or unpredictable, it can be terrifying to expose a need to God, who might not come through. But even the best parental relationships only hint at what God longs to provide. Although our human relationships will always be flawed, the comfort of God is perfect. And trustworthy. How has your human experience of comfort impacted your expectation (or lack thereof) of comfort from God? Allow the truth of the Bible to rewrite what you believe about God's offer to comfort you.

Day 47

I Am Delivered

I have told you these things, so that in me you may have peace. In this world you will have trouble. But take heart! I have overcome the world.

—*John 16:33*

The storm hit hard and fast and without warning.

Several hours before, we'd loaded kids and adults into our family boat for a day of skiing and tubing on Las Vegas' Lake Mead. The day started in perfection. Blue sky dotted with cotton clouds. Bright sun reflecting on glasslike waters.

It was the first time we'd taken my niece out on the boat. Only three years old, she took it all in with wide-eyed wonder. When she watched her daddy—my brother—playing on the tube, she giggled in delight.

But the laughter died the moment the storm struck. Cotton clouds turned ominous. Glasslike waters turned foamy and whitecapped. With a glance at the shore, I knew it would take more than a few minutes to get to safety. But with each second, the swells grew, threatening to overcome our tiny boat.

I reached for my niece, pulled her onto my lap, and held her close while my husband kept his hands white-knuckled on the wheel. To drive directly to shore, we had to steer straight into the gale-force wind. But to drive into the wind in this monstrous storm meant a risk of capsizing. We needed to get off the water. But how?

I closed my eyes and prayed. As my three-year-old niece gripped my arms, my heart reached for the God I knew could deliver us.

Save us, God!

I hoped for a Jesus-sized miracle, like the day He spoke to a Sea of Galilee storm, and wind and waves came to a dead stop (Mark 4:39).

But our storm continued. In spite of my faith-filled prayers, Jesus didn't deliver. If anything, the wind grew in intensity. I tried to stay calm for the kids, but my heart pounded with fear. I grew up on boats, knew a storm or two. But nothing like this one. Not even close.

While my brother navigated from the bow in an effort to keep the boat balanced, my husband started cutting *z* formations in the water. Turning left, then right kept him from driving straight into the wind. As a result, we inched closer to the shore.

Our nightmare lasted about an hour, a lifetime to a family who thought they might drown. Soaked and cold, weak from fear, we pulled ourselves and our boat out of the water and made for the safety of home. There I could finally contemplate my nagging questions: Why didn't God deliver us? Why didn't He calm the storm? I knew He was more than able; I believed it to my core. Thus the reason I prayed, because I knew my God could deliver.

And still the storm raged, oblivious to my request.

Even so. We made it home.

It took years for the lesson to have its full impact on my heart. For a long time I wondered why some storm-prayers are answered with calm and others are not. But now I see that day on Lake Mead a bit differently: Sometimes God delivers us *from* a storm. But other times He delivers us *in* it.

That day on the lake, God gave my husband the wisdom to *z* his way back to shore. God kept the boat balanced in waves far bigger than it could handle. And He kept all our children and family members wrapped up in life vests and out of the water. He didn't still the storm. But He calmed my kids and gave us a great story to tell our friends.

To those praying for a Deliverer, John 10:10 records Jesus making a powerful proclamation: "I have come that they may have life, and have it to the full."

I always loved that verse, probably because it sounded like the promise of a happy life. Naively, I believed Jesus' words included protection from all harm. Like a divine umbrella, God would spread the expanse of His arms over me and my loved ones and keep us from all rain.

It didn't take long to end up soaking wet.

But that's when I remembered more of Jesus' words, only six chapters later in John 16:33: "In this world you will have trouble."

Not "might have trouble." Not "could have trouble."

"In this world you *will* have trouble."

It's not a matter of if; it's a matter of when.

The same Jesus who promised deliverance also promised trouble. At first glance, Jesus' words sound contradictory. And yet His life proves otherwise. It was His death that made possible our lives. Hardship to realize hope. Trouble today for the promise of a party tomorrow.

Can I trust Jesus to deliver me through one to arrive at the other?

The unexpected is unavoidable. My dream of a trouble-free life was more than a little far-fetched. It doesn't matter whether you live in an affluent suburb of upper-class America or in an overcrowded slum of poverty-stricken India. The rain falls on each of us in good measure.

The question, then, is this: do you trust the Deliverer?

He's the hiding place, the shelter in the rain. Yes, there are moments when God delivers you and me from our troubles. Children overcome obstacles, illnesses are healed, marriages are revived.

But more often than not, He doesn't deliver us from harm; He delivers us *in* it. The first is merely protection. The second is presence. The first causes us to cringe, as we wait for the next calamity to fall. The second provides a harbor of rest, regardless of the weather.

Life is more than calm and predictable circumstances. Life—full life—is weathering the unexpected storms and the impossible waves knowing the Deliverer is present with you in them.

We will read our story by the light of redemption and see how God has used both the good and the bad, the sorrow and the gladness for our welfare and his glory.

—Brent Curtis and John Eldredge, *The Sacred Romance*

Who Am I?

Consider both God's deliverance from the storm and God's deliverance in the storm. If possible, think of an example of each in your life. Each scenario holds the potential to teach different, yet valuable, lessons. What did you learn (or are you learning) from each? If you're in a storm, consider that God might deliver you in ways you don't expect. What could be the hidden treasure in your dark place?

Day 48

I Am

He has sent me to proclaim freedom for the prisoners and recovery of sight for the blind, to set the oppressed free.

—*Luke 4:18*

Only those who know captivity understand the gift of being set free. Ask Louie Zamperini, the World War II airman who crashed in the Pacific Ocean and spent forty-seven days adrift on a raft before being captured and imprisoned as a Japanese POW.

As I said. Ask Louie.

I read his story in Laura Hillenbrand's bestselling book *Unbroken* years before Hollywood and Angelina Jolie made it into a feature film. It took me only a handful of days to finish it, captivated as I was by both Zamperini's courage and his pain. I'll never forget the tension I felt with every page turn. At times I wanted to put the book down, to pull away. His was a story saturated with suffering. Yet lessons and revelations filled every page. I kept reading. Even when it was hard.

Some could say Louie, when he was a child, was a slave to his angst. Impulsive and conflicted, he landed in trouble more often than not. But then, with the help of his brother, he discovered he had a gift for running.

Soon he redirected all that childhood energy to the track oval, where he worked out his inner conflict in competition.

Then came World War II. A plane crash. A life raft. A POW camp. Too many days a slave to circumstance.

Louie's captivity came in various forms. A slave to impulsivity, a slave to fear, a slave to survival, a slave to a persecutor, to name just a few. However, I imagine Louie would tell you, if he were still alive, that the final chains of captivity were the toughest to break.

The chains of unforgiveness.

It was when he carried home with him the memories of mistreatment at the hands of his enemy that Louie found himself consumed by bitterness. He wanted to exact revenge on those who'd made him suffer. His captors still held him hostage, even from thousands of miles away. It took a Billy Graham sermon and the powerful pull of the Holy Spirit to break Louie free.

I've never been in jail nor have I ever been handcuffed. I don't know what it feels like to carry the weight of a prison sentence or spend a sleepless night in a cell. But I do know what it feels like to be bound by history, regret, and hurt I refuse to release. And to feel justified clinging to chains of my own making.

In the long run, that which I believe will justify me instead ends up enslaving me.

I may not have any experience with horrific confinement on an ocean raft, but I do know what it's like to be stuck in a sea of bitterness for far longer than forty-seven days. When a close friend questioned my integrity several years ago, I felt betrayed. The circumstances surrounding the situation were insignificant, trivial. And yet emotion turned a simple misunderstanding into a sharp character assault. I reeled from the blow. I thought she knew me. She was my friend, after all. How could she doubt my heart? And yet she did. No benefit of the doubt, no honest dialogue. Just a painful accusation our friendship couldn't weather.

Day 48

It took far more than forty-seven days for me to let the hurt go. Even a year or two later, I still felt the sting of it from time to time. It was unfair, and I struggled to forgive it.

And what about that time when I failed to show up for another friend? She needed me. She'd asked me to come, to help her through a crisis that weighed her down. Instead, I got caught up in my own lesser crises, allowed myself to be preoccupied by responsibilities and tasks that could've been put off for another day. By the time I'd recognized my selfishness, I'd missed an opportunity. I tried to make it up to her, to own my mistake, apologize and reschedule our time together. But I couldn't get past the fact that I'd failed her. In her moment of need, I'd blown it. It was unforgiveable.

Yes, like Louie, I know what it's like to be enslaved by unforgiveness and to be chained to regrets and failures. Whether my grievance is aimed at others or myself, I feel unable to let go.

Then I remember: "Freely you have received; freely give," Jesus said (Matt. 10:8). It's that simple. And that hard.

True freedom isn't being free to do what you want, say what you want, live how you want. You could call that independence, perhaps. But being a slave to myself is simply exchanging one type of slavery for another. Instead, true freedom comes when we chain ourselves to something truer and more trustworthy than ourselves. When we attach ourselves to someone who sets the standard for everything good and pure and beautiful.

Then, as slaves to true freedom, we turn around and offer to others a portion of the grace we've been given. Including ourselves.

In Galatians 5:1, Paul said it this way: "It is for freedom that Christ has set us free. Stand firm, then, and do not let yourselves be burdened again by a yoke of slavery." Our Father has already set us free. Our forgiveness has been bought and paid for, absolving our failures and all those who've failed us. We forget sometimes, returning to the regrets and wounds that feel far too familiar.

Instead, we can ask the giver of freedom to help us see the chains for what they are, a return to the slavery from which we've been freed. May our only captivity be in living as a slave to Him.

The most liberating act of free, unconditional love demands that the recipient give up control of his or her life. Is that a contradiction? No . . . It is only grace that frees us from the slavery of self that lurks even in the middle of morality and religion.

—Timothy Keller, *The Reason for God*

Who Am I?

Unforgiveness only enslaves the person clinging to it. It does nothing to the person who exacted the wrongdoing. And yet unforgiveness is so difficult to shed. We hang on to our wounds as if they're the only means of self-preservation. Consider any remnants of unforgiveness in your heart. Be ruthlessly honest, knowing that your freedom lies on the other side. What injustices or regrets are you struggling to release? Ask the one who set you free to show you, in shocking clarity, the cost of your unforgiveness. Then ask Him to give you the strength to let your chains go, once and for all. Make us free, Father God! Make us free.

Day 49

I Am *Empowered*

Truly I tell you, if you have faith as small as a mustard seed, you can say to this mountain, "Move from here to there" and it will move. Nothing will be impossible for you.

—*Matthew 17:20*

The gift arrived when I least expected it. And when I most needed it. A small corked jar, no bigger than a thimble. Filled with dozens of yellow-brown mustard seeds, each smaller than the head of a pin.

For months, I'd been struggling with my faith. After too many years of physical pain, I came up for a brief reprieve only to face a vast sea of spiritual pain. For nearly five years, I'd prayed for God to deliver me from cancer and suffering, to restore my life to health and protect my family from further heartache. Beyond my own prayers, thousands of friends and family and strangers offered up theirs. Add it all up and it equaled far more than a thimble jar filled with faith.

Even so, illness and death continued to stalk me. In spite of my pleas, God didn't seem inclined to intervene.

What about my mustard seed of faith, God? I thought You said it was enough.

With books and Bibles and journals gathered around me, I searched for answers and wrestled with the God I'd always loved. I still loved Him, still believed in Him. I just didn't understand Him. I didn't understand His promise of power coupled with His apparent unwillingness to deliver it. We'd prayed. Fasted. Believed promises and memorized Bible verses.

Where was God?

Thus, my friend, Traci, sent mustard seeds. A Matthew 17:20 reminder for the girl who feared her fragile faith and nagging doubts meant she was a terrible Christian after all. With one glance at her thimble-sized jar, I remembered: it isn't the size of a girl's faith but the presence of it that counts.

I wonder if the disciples experienced a similar angst when their best efforts to heal a boy came up short. They'd been given power to heal diseases and cast out demons. By that point, they'd done it enough times to feel a measure of confidence that healing would come once again.

Only it didn't. No matter how many times they tried. So the boy's father asked Jesus for help, and Jesus came through. When the disciples asked why their efforts didn't produce results, Jesus said simply, "Because you have so little faith" (Matt. 17:20).

So little faith? I'm confused. It seems to me they had far more faith than most.

But the disciples' shortage of faith wasn't a lack of belief in the power of God. They knew Jesus was able. They didn't doubt His reality or capability.

But their expectation wasn't sourced in relationship. They'd failed to submit their will to the will of their Father. Only there, in full submission, is a mustard seed of faith a powerful mountain-moving thing.

I do not know why some mountains move and others remain firmly in place. I've seen people of tall and true faith baffled by God's lack of response. And I've seen people stuck in a mire of doubt and unbelief surprised by a miracle their faith doesn't seem to deserve. I know that belief and faith are critical pieces of this spiritual journey to the glory of heaven. But I also know that Jesus believed fully in God's ability to deliver when He begged for deliverance the night before His death. He had more than a thimble-sized jar of faith, and yet God chose not to move His mountain.

Or, perhaps, His mountain moved after all. In the size and shape of a tomb-sealing stone. In a moment, faith moved it from here to there, and the Son of God walked out, alive.

No, God didn't move the mountain of His crucifixion. But God moved the mountain of His death in a beautiful resurrection.

I don't claim to have all the answers, nor can I unravel the mysteries of our unfathomable God. But perhaps the greatest faith, a mountain-moving faith, is one that bends low. One that submits to the will of the Father and allows the power of God to move in ways we wouldn't have imagined.

In our tiniest mustard seed of faith, we too have access to that kind of power. When we bow our desires to the plan of a God we love and trust, we have access to a far greater power than we've ever known. Resurrection power. The same power that raised Jesus from the dead is in you and in me. That means when we pray for mountains to move, they move. Sometimes it's the mountain right in front of us. Other times, it's the bigger mountain we don't yet see.

I still pray for healing, hoping God will grant my heart's desire. I still pray for a body that's renewed and a life that's long.

But I also pray those healing prayers on bent knees, knowing God may choose to move a mountain bigger than this one.

Either way, I can trust Him to empower me. Even if all I can muster up is a mustard seed of faith.

We are not always sure where the horizon is. We would not know "which end is up" were it not for the shimmering pathway of light falling on the white sea. The One who laid earth's foundations and settled its dimensions knows where the lines are drawn. He gives all the light we need for trust and for obedience.

—Elisabeth Elliot, *Through Gates of Splendor*

Who Am I?

To be empowered by God means we've been given a strength far beyond our human capacity. We're given physical strength, emotional strength, spiritual strength. God's resurrection power lives within us through the presence and working of the Holy Spirit. That right there is a mountain-moving power. Do you ever wrestle with unanswered prayer and the promise of God's power? How does Jesus' prayer struggle in the garden of Gethsemane help bring a measure of peace to you?

Day 50

I Am Redeemed

I have swept away your offenses like a cloud, your sins like the morning mist. Return to me, for I have redeemed you.

—Isaiah 44:22

I like to think of myself as an easy-to-please wife.

(But let's not invite my husband into this conversation, shall we?)

I don't need fancy cars or houses. For Christmas and birthdays, I prefer homemade gifts, handwritten notes, and time spent together more than anything purchased. I'm not much of a shopper, nor do I like going out to eat. When it comes to date nights, all I need is one night a month and a babysitter who covers the bedtime routine. Amen, hallelujah. And rather than fancy dinners and dancing lessons, I'd just as soon go out for buffalo wings and a ballgame.

However, if my husband was to give me the gift of all gifts, it would be this: a promise to take a long walk with me once a week.

An easy-to-please wife, right?

However. Taking walks is not my husband's thing. Not at all. I could fill up page after page of ways he cares for me and serves me without the slightest complaint. But going for a walk? He'd rather have all his teeth and toenails pulled out. At the same time.

All this is to say, for nearly two decades, I've asked this precious man of mine to go for a walk with me. After nearly two decades, I can count on one hand the number of times that little dream has come true.

Which is why last Valentine's Day surprised me. Along with a perfect bouquet of red roses waiting for me when I came down the stairs, I also found a sealed envelope with a card inside. Inside the card was a handmade certificate. From my husband. For one long walk. Together.

Glory. I don't know what got into that man, but I wasn't going to knock it. I saved that certificate for just the right day, just the right evening, when we could take a walk together during a spectacular Colorado sunset. I couldn't wait to cash in my card. The redemption was the sweetest part of the gift.

We know this, right? Every time we receive a gift card or a gift certificate, we don't get excited about the piece of plastic or the thin piece of paper. We're excited about what the card or certificate represents. What we hold in our hands isn't the offering but a promise of the redemption yet to come.

To redeem means to make an exchange. A coupon for a latte. A certificate for a massage. A gift card for a $200 shopping spree at our favorite store. What we hold in our hands will eventually be redeemed for something far better than a piece of paper or plastic.

When it comes to my life, there are too many parts I wish I could redeem for something better. For example:

- A difficult season of marriage for an easy, conflict-free one.
- A painful memory for a happy one.
- A past mistake for a second chance.
- A middle-aged body for a younger one.
- Graying hair for hair that stays its original color forever and ever, amen.

I digress.

My point is this: all of us would like to make a few exchanges if we could. We'd like to experience a redemption of our circumstances for a promise of something much better yet to come.

But no matter how much I'd like that exchange to be made, it's usually impossible. I can't go back in time and take back a harsh word or undo a reckless decision. I can't redeem my years of untried parenting for my current hard-earned experience. I can't erase my many sins and flaws for a whole and righteous life.

Unless.

Unless I relinquish my flawed life to hands that can redeem it.

"So I went down to the potter's house, and I saw him working at the wheel. But the pot he was shaping from the clay was marred in his hands; so the potter formed it into another pot, shaping it as seemed best to him. Then the word of the LORD came to me. He said, 'Can I not do with you, Israel, as this potter does?' declares the LORD. 'Like clay in the hand of the potter, so are you in my hand, Israel'" (Jer. 18:3–6).

What is marred in my hands becomes pottery in progress in His. To me, the form and shape of my life look irreparable. To the Potter? He sees an opportunity to show off His best work. All of it is redeemable. The impossible and imperfect, the broken and beat up. Nothing is wasted in His expert hands as He remakes us into something beautiful.

He doesn't remove our flaws. He redeems them.

He doesn't bury the past. He uses it.

Beauty for ashes, gladness for mourning, praise for despair (Isa. 61:1–4).

Why? Because it shows off His glory.

And because He loves nothing more than to take a long walk with us, flaws and all.

God is absolutely sovereign . . . He rejoices in all His works when He contemplates them as colors of the magnificent mosaic of redemptive history. He is an unshakably happy God.

—John Piper, *Desiring God*

Who Am I?

I have no doubt that God has already done some powerful redemption work in your life. Consider the unexpected gifts that have come from your mistakes, doubts, questions, and rebellions. Then read Psalm 103. Make a list as you read the psalmist's words of the many ways God has redeemed you and your story

Part 6

REVELATION

Day 51

I Am Rewarded

For whoever wants to save their life will lose it, but whoever loses their life for me will find it.

—Matthew 16:25

It's a difficult tension living with one foot on earth and the other reaching for heaven.

Perhaps that's why, for the majority of my life, I kept both feet firmly planted on earth.

It's not that I didn't think about eternity. When a pastor preached on the subject or I read a Bible verse about heaven or I attended a funeral, I'd give mortality a passing glance. I knew the end would one day come. But the knowing didn't seem to change the living, at least not too much. Who wants to spend her life thinking about death? A morose way to live, I thought.

Until death knocked on my door.

Then I didn't have much of a choice.

In spite of my attempts to shove thoughts of death and dying to the side, they wouldn't be ignored. For thirty-nine years, I lived as if ignorant of the guarantee of death. Overnight, it became the only thing I could think about.

Day 51

Thus began a year or two of desperate attempts to preserve my life. I changed my diet and added more exercise. I avoided toxic candles and cleaning supplies, and I signed up for weekly yoga. When I wasn't searching the internet and talking to doctors about various cures, I prayed like a fasting monk for God to deliver a mountain-moving miracle.

Then death knocked on my door a second time. And a third.

Suddenly all those years of self-preservation efforts seemed silly. Futile. And something occurred to me: the numbering of my days here on earth isn't up to me; it's up to the one who numbered them long before I was born.

Job, a man well acquainted with pain and suffering, found comfort in this assurance: "A person's days are determined; you have decreed the number of his months and have set limits he cannot exceed" (Job 14:5).

If Job's words are true, then all my efforts to save myself were nothing more than futile attempts to play God. There's nothing wrong with being a good steward of life and health, of treating this gift of life with humility and care. But in the end, I mustn't forget: I'm not God; He is.

But I learned something else during those desperate months contemplating death. In all my obsession with this life, I'd failed to celebrate the next one. I'd forgotten that the real gift isn't our humanity; it's eternity. That's the reward we're waiting for.

Our human nature hosts an incredible will to live. I've seen friends plagued with pain fight for years before taking their last breath. We have such determination to overcome, a survival mechanism that keeps us pressing on when we want to quit.

But this gift was never meant to eclipse a greater one. Eternity is the ultimate reward. And the only way to receive that gift is to let the lesser gift go.

On the island of Patmos, God gave John, one of the twelve disciples of Jesus, a revelation of the reward to come. John received it with both trembling and joy, experiencing and then recording his visions of the second coming of our Christ. Justice for wrongdoing. Redemption for the repentant. And an eternity absent tears in the presence of absolute glory.

Too often, however, I'm so caught up in my daily life that I miss the sweetness of my eternal one. Like a toddler so enamored with wrapping paper that he misses the thrill of a new toy, I only have eyes for this life and miss the beauty of the one yet to come. But as Jesus said, "To the one who is victorious, I will give the right to sit with me on my throne" (Rev. 3:21). This is the reward we're waiting for. If we give this life to Him, there is a new and better life waiting for us.

Perhaps we don't spend enough time talking to each other about heaven. It feels too far off and distant, hard for a human mind to comprehend. And yet talking about it also creates appreciation for it, not to mention no small amount of anticipation.

Yes, it's difficult living with one foot on earth and the other reaching for heaven. And yet it's the only way to truly live. Want to save your life? Go ahead and spend every effort in desperate preservation. It won't matter, you know. One day we'll have to face the fact this life was never really ours to save.

Instead, trust the one who already knows the number of your days, and life—real life—will be waiting for you. Steward this life, yes. But don't fail to be a joyful dreamer of heaven. The real reward isn't what's in front of you. The reward is what is yet to come.

Keep yourself as a stranger here on earth, a pilgrim whom its affairs do not concern at all. Keep your heart free and raise it up to God, for you have not here a lasting home. To Him direct your daily prayers, your sighs and tears, that your soul may merit after death to pass in happiness to the Lord.

—Thomas á Kempis, *The Imitation of Christ*

Day 51

Who Am I?

The Bible indicates that much of this life—including creation—hints at the new heaven and new earth that are yet to come. I believe the evidences for eternity are all around us. Today be intentional about searching for hints of heaven. Ask God to open your eyes to see what you might otherwise miss, and then write down what you discover in a journal. How does this change your perspective on this imperfect life?

Day 52

I Am Renewed

I will refresh the weary and satisfy the faint.
—*Jeremiah* 31:25

Recently I found out a dear friend is on hospice. Her years of fighting breast cancer to no avail, she now faces the imminent end of her life.

My heart hurts.

Over the years of our friendship, I've watched her face her foe with joy and unwavering belief in her God. Her spirit—even in her real moments of struggle—gave me courage when I faced my own life-and-death battle. It gives me strength still.

And yet tonight my heart feels only grief. No strength. No confidence. No courage, spiritual or otherwise. Only a sadness that seeps into my bones and a weariness that will not be relieved. I know a bit of her suffering. I know the kind of physical pain that makes you wish for death. I understand the exhaustion of soul that can't stand the thought of another five minutes of life.

Today she endures that—and so much more.

So tonight I think about her, hovering on the edge of death. And to tell you the truth, it exhausts me. I'm tired of this broken and fragile life. I'm tired of the suffering that seems determined to torture us. I'm tired of the lack of relief, the absence of answers. Today, as seems to happen more often than not, I feel like a desperate King David, weeping tears that refuse to comfort:

> *My heart is in anguish within me;*
> *The terrors of death have fallen on me.*
> *Fear and trembling have beset me;*
> *horror has overwhelmed me.*
> *I said, "Oh, that I had the wings of a dove!*
> *I would fly away and be at rest.*
> *I would flee far away and stay in the desert;*
> *I would hurry to my place of shelter,*
> *far from the tempest and storm.*
>
> —Psalm 55:4–8

> *I sink in the miry depths,*
> *where there is no foothold.*
> *I have come into the deep waters;*
> *The floods engulf me.*
> *I am worn out calling for help;*
> *my throat is parched.*
> *My eyes fail,*
> *looking for my God.*
>
> —Psalm 69:2–3

It's not that I don't believe in God. I do—with all my heart. But this human spirit is not indomitable. Like a towel washed too many times, I feel I've grown too thin.

In an attempt to pull myself from my despair, I opened my computer to check email. Waiting for me, like a hand-delivered gift, was a message from Chris, an online friend who lives in Germany. He too knows a thing or two about physical suffering. Having endured multiple life-threatening illnesses requiring brutal and constant treatment, he experiences long stretches of days during which he cannot pull his twenty-nine-year-old self out of bed. Not easy for a man accustomed to a high-paced corporate job, running marathons, and enjoying an adventurous life. Without knowing my sadness, he'd sent me the following words: "To inspire (used nonreflexively), from the Latin *inspirare*, has of course the stem *spir* in it. It is, very literally, to give or put spirit into someone. To inspire someone is way more than making them happy or amazed or even making them feel good. It is to lend them spirit when they are short. And of course because of the incorporeal nature of both air and spirit, the act of inhaling also became known as inspiration. In that sense too: it is like mechanical ventilation for a soul that's lost its resolve for a moment."

After that, he told me that my hard journey inspires his own, even when I don't realize it. What he didn't know, couldn't know, is that with a few words dashed off in an email, Chris offered mechanical ventilation in a moment when I could no longer inhale any hope for myself.

More than that, however, my friend's words reminded me of another gift of inspiration:

> But when the kindness and love of God our Savior appeared, he saved us, not because of righteous things we had done, but because of his mercy. He saved us through the washing of rebirth and renewal by the Holy Spirit, whom he poured out on us generously.
>
> —*Titus 3:4–6*

> Not only so, but we also glory in our sufferings, because we know that suffering produces perseverance; perseverance, character; and character, hope. And hope does not put us to shame, because God's love has been poured out into our hearts through the Holy Spirit, who has been given to us.
>
> —*Romans 5:3–5*

Day 52

In a world that flings around the word inspiration without a thought, we've been offered the only real gift of inspiration mankind could ever hope for: the Holy Spirit. The presence of God exhaling hope into us.

God has breathed into you and me the breath of life, so that when hard moments come and we no longer have the strength to inhale on our own, we can trust He'll renew our weary souls.

Inhale. Exhale. Grief may last for a night, but joy comes in the morning.

Can you feel the freedom that rises up in you when you have been stripped naked and have nothing to inhibit your movement anymore? . . . Jesus enters into our sadness, takes us by the hand, pulls us grently up to where we can stand and invites us to dance.

—Henri J.M. Nouwen, *Spiritual Formation*

Who Am I?

Read Romans 5:3–5 again. According to Paul's words, the road to hope often travels through suffering. Relief comes only to those feeling pain. Renewal comes only as a result of our needing to be renewed. Hope comes only as a result of needing hope. Does this alter your perspective on suffering, perseverance, and the building of character? If your soul is weary and your heart heavy, invite the Breath of Life to exhale deeply into your soul. You don't have to have the strength to breathe on your own. Instead, inhale. Divine ventilation is yours.

Day 53

I Am Radiant

Then you will look and be radiant, your heart will throb and swell with joy.

—Isaiah 60:5

Apparently, we can now buy radiance in a bottle.

This is good news for those of us who woke up today only to discover we're no longer fifteen. A glance in my own mirror this morning revealed more age spots and dark circles than a Dalmatian.

Radiance? Yes, please.

Aveeno markets their Positively Radiant skin care line with promises to "improve skin tone and radiance with clinically proven Total Soy Complex."

If Aveeno isn't your thing, you could go with L'Oreal. They have a RevitaLift Radiant Smoothing Cream Cleanser that "helps to remove all traces of makeup and impurities . . . gently exfoliates dead skin cells and helps enhance skin smoothness and radiance."

Or how about Maybelline's Instant Age Rewind Radiant Firming Makeup? I can shine, tighten, *and* take a decade off my aging-and-sagging self. All for the low price of $8.99.

Day 53

Well, there you go. Radiance for less than ten bucks. I'll take twelve.

If only it worked. After much trial and error, I'm disappointed to report that none of the grandiose promises of the skin care market actually come true. A little moisturizer can do a girl (or guy) a world of good. But deliver radiance? I don't think so.

Besides, I've met individuals who didn't wear a stitch of makeup, yet light spilled from every pore. Something about their smile, the twinkle in their eyes, the peace of their demeanor delivered a unique glow.

And what is radiance, anyway? By definition, radiance is "a quality of brightness and happiness that can be seen on a person's face; a warm, soft light that shines from something." Inherent in the definition is the idea that the glow comes from an intense source, often a reflection of something outside of itself.

Like a pool deck radiating the heat of the summer sun.

Or the smooth surface of a lake reflecting the silver light of the moon.

Or, in the Old Testament, the face of Moses shining with the magnificent glory of his God.

The book of Exodus tells the story. At God's invitation, Moses climbed Mount Sinai, where he spent forty days and forty nights in His presence (Ex. 24:18). During that time, God gave him the law His people were to follow (v. 12). From their distant camp, the Israelites saw the glory of God covering the mountain with a cloud. At the end of those forty days and nights, Moses once again descended Mount Sinai and rejoined his people. That's when they noticed something remarkable about their man: "When Moses came down from Mount Sinai with the two tablets of the covenant law in his hands, he was not aware that his face was radiant because he had spoken with the Lord. When Aaron and all the Israelites saw Moses, his face was radiant, and they were afraid to come near him" (34:29–30).

Talk about a good makeup job! Spending time in God's presence sparked a transformation of Moses' face. Luminosity in its purest form.

Bright enough to make everyone else afraid. That's some serious radiance. Even more beautiful, Moses' shine came secondary to his deep soul-hunger for God:

- "If you are pleased with me, teach me your ways so I may know you and continue to find favor with you" (33:13).
- "If your Presence does not go with us, do not send us up from here" (33:15).
- "The LORD would speak to Moses face to face, as one speaks with a friend" (33:11).

Oh, how I want to be the friend of God! To speak to the Lord face to face . . . I can hardly imagine it.

Moses' kinship with his Creator was the source of his luminosity. Isn't this the same gift we've been given? Paul, with the perspective of the New Testament, said this: "And we all, who with unveiled faces contemplate the Lord's glory, are being transformed into his image with ever-increasing glory, which comes from the Lord, who is the Spirit" (2 Cor. 3:18).

The short of it is this: the more you and I spend time with our God, the more we reflect His radiance. Like a lake reflects the moon, or a face the sun. This is how some people, regardless of hardship and loss, can still shine. They don't rely on manufactured radiance; they go to the source: the glory of God.

This is what I'm holding out for as I age and my beauty fades. I've grown weary of second-rate attempts at shine. I don't want eight-dollar radiance. I want to glow with an otherworldly glory. I want to be like Moses, to spend my days soaking up the Light of Life, and thus become a reflection of Him. Glowing with a shine that can't be washed off.

Radiance, of the divine variety? Free and guaranteed?

Yes, please. I'll take me some of that.

Day 53

It is only because he became like us that we can become like him.

—Dietrich Bonhoeffer, *The Cost of Discipleship*

Who Am I?

Although the radiance of God comes at no monetary cost, it still has a price: time in God's presence. Too often, however, we'd rather spend thirty or forty dollars on beauty that washes off than fifteen or thirty minutes in the Light of Life Himself. Revelation 21:23 says, "The city does not need the sun or the moon to shine on it, for the glory of God gives it light, and the Lamb is its lamp." This is a glimpse of what happens when God's presence fills a place. How much radiance do you need? How much do you *want*?

Day 54

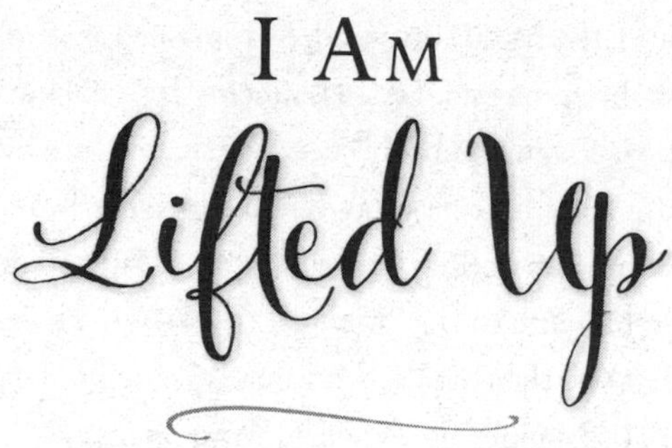

Blessed are you who weep now, for you will laugh.

—*Luke 6:21*

He was five months old and quite possibly the most precious, cheek-kissable baby I'd ever seen.

My friend had brought him with her to our conference, attached as he was to regular three-hour feedings. From the moment I saw his cherubic face, I felt the impulse to make him laugh. Seriously, is there anything more yummy than baby laughter? As a mama of teenagers and grade-schoolers, I hadn't heard any of that goodness for far too long.

Thus began my descent into shameless grown-up theatrics. Awkward dancing. Gawking smiles. Strawberries, baby talk, and spit bubbles.

You name it, I tried it. A valiant effort to spark a giggle. However, the cherub would not give in to a grin. He extended his lower lip far enough to provide a table for dinner and then burst into a gut-wrenching cry.

I tried not to take it personally, despite the fact that moments before, his mama had declared him the happiest of her four babies. Really.

Day 54

Happiest baby award aside, he wasn't the least bit impressed with me. Clearly I was out of my league.

"Oh, it's not you," she reassured me. "He needs a new diaper."

Well, now. That would make even the happiest of us cranky.

But moments later, freshly diapered, he remained as cranky as before. He needed a nap, his mom said. I tried bouncing and rocking and walking him to no avail. He fought against his need for sleep. Until his mom came near. Lifting him from his carrier and high above her head, she offered soothing words and her smiling, reassuring face. Up and down, up and down, she lifted him into the air. And just that fast, her sweet, tired boy started to smile. And then giggle. And finally, outright laugh.

Hallelujah! His laughter lit my world. And his.

A few days ago, I sat with a close friend who's enduring unthinkable loss. The details don't matter; most of us understand without explanation the agony of losing something precious. As we sat only feet apart, I asked her what she needed most. Through tears, she listed things like prayer and companionship, which I expected. And gladly offered. But she needed something more.

"I need to laugh. It's been so long since I've done that."

Yes, of course. That made perfect sense. I've known that need myself.

"There is a time for everything," Solomon said. "A time to weep and a time to laugh, a time to mourn and a time to dance" (Eccl. 3:1, 4).

The times of weeping and laughing often go together, don't they?

As a woman who has struggled too long with significant illness, I know about long seasons of laughterless weeping. Tears that won't stop no matter your efforts to hold them back. The lamentation of a broken heart makes laughter appear too far out of reach. I too have known seasons when I'd forgotten what laughter feels like.

Until, somehow, God lifted me from my circumstances and up into the air. Smiling and reassuring, He offered a moment of relief, laughter in my tears.

My children dressing the dog in Superman underwear.

My husband's dry and well-timed quips.

Our chaotic ordinary life that often reads like a comedy script.

God has a knack for delivering laughter when I least expect it. And many times He delivers it in the middle of my bad mood. It doesn't last forever, but it's long enough for a little relief.

More than a promise of earthly levity, I believe Jesus' words in Luke 6 are actually about a greater joy yet to come. Like we know our earthly tears, we will know the kind of laughter that refuses to be stifled. The temporary laughter of this life is merely a hint of the perfected joy yet to come. Matthew Henry says it this way: "They that now sorrow after a godly sort are treasuring up comforts for themselves, or, rather, God is treasuring up comforts for them; and the day is coming when their mouth shall be filled with laughing and their lips with rejoicing, Job 8:21."[9]

The laughter of God is far more about what is to come than what is. The real joy, I know, is being stored up for us in heaven, in an eternal destination absent tears and filled with a deluge of laughter we won't be able to contain. I can't wait, can you?

Until then, you and I will often sit a few feet from friends and exchange stories that cause us both to weep. Even so, remember: "When these things begin to take place, stand up and lift up your heads, because your redemption is drawing near" (Luke 21:28).

I was to discover, however, that when I took my eyes off the circumstances that were overwhelming me, over which I had no control, and looked up, my Lord was there, standing on the parapet of heaven looking down. Deep in my heart He whispered, "I'm here. Even when you don't see Me, I'm here. Never for a moment are you out of My sight."

—Darlene Deibler Rose, *Evidence Not Seen*

Day 54

Who Am I?

How long has it been since you laughed? What were the circumstances surrounding your joy? For those of you who can't remember your last moment of laughter, have no fear. We can easily become so buried by our troubles that we forget to create moments of spontaneity and fun. First, pray the words of Psalm 126:1–6. Invite God to spark fresh laughter in your heart. Then, before the day is done, *play.* Eat ice cream for dinner. Dance to music in the family room. Watch a comedy or start a tickle fight. The method doesn't matter as much as making joy part of your day.

Day 55

I Am Honored

The L*ORD* *will be your everlasting light, and your God will be your glory.*

—ISAIAH 60:19

Each year when the Academy Awards roll around, my friend Robbie throws a party. Themed food, a large television, and a house filled with friends and anticipation as we await the start of the big show. Adding to the drama, she creates a competition of sorts, with each person attempting to guess the various winners, the best dresses, the most memorable moments.

Although I'm not much of an Oscar watcher, I admit I'm easily caught up in the glamour. I imagine myself in a sequined dress with an expert updo and borrowed jewels. I wait for the announcer to say my name, winner of an award. Then when I hear it, I fake cry, relinquish my seat, and walk to the stage while soaking in the applause and affirmation of my peers.

Welcome to the fantasy world of a middle-aged woman. For the record, I'm fully aware this will never happen. But a girl can dream. What would it be like to be so honored? I can't even get my children to mutter the occasional, "Thanks for the way you tirelessly work your arthritic fingers to a nub so we can have a life of ease."

Not that I hold unrealistic expectations.

It's sweet to be seen. To be honored for our contributions, with or without the sequined dress and jewels.

Several months ago, my third boy graduated from high school. Before the big day, we received an invitation in the mail.

"Senior Awards Ceremony," it said. Our son had received some kind of award, and we were invited to the celebration.

The night was beautiful in many ways. Jacob, eighteen years old and looking forward to a future in the United States Air Force, received a Historian Award for his excellence in history. In addition, he received an engineering honor as well as other academic and athletic honors.

But it wasn't the awards that made the evening wonderful. It was the backstory leading up to it.

In our two-plus decades as parents, my husband and I have been blessed with countless amazing teachers and administrators during our children's school years. Including Jacob's.

But among the many positive influences, there were a few who couldn't see the potential we saw. Instead, they looked at our in-progress boy and saw a talkative, impulsive, bundle of too much energy. Many times, this tension made Jacob's early school years tough and emotional. The hardest part? He knew. Even at five, seven, or twelve years old, he knew the teachers who didn't like him, who couldn't see the good in him. He felt their doubt and disapproval.

Then the Senior Awards Ceremony. And it turns out a little boy with excessive energy can grow up to be a young man with a sharp intellect. And an impulsive, talkative little boy can grow into an amazing leader ready to serve and change the world. Proof that what you see in your baby today is only a fraction of the man or woman they'll become tomorrow.

As I watched him accept his award, as I blinked back tears and thought of both the naysayers and the cheerleaders, I couldn't help but reflect that God alone is our biggest fan. Only God looks at our in-progress selves and sees a person worth honoring, regardless of her accomplishments.

You and I will likely never appear on the Oscar stage. I'll never get a golden statue for doing an impressive stack of dinner dishes, and I'm far too old for any Senior Awards Ceremonies.

Unless, of course, it's the Senior Living Facility Awards. But let's not go there.

There's an Oscar-worthy performance we're a part of nonetheless. It's called history and the redemption of mankind. From the beginning of time, God has set out to rescue His people. It's a story of love lost, love pursued, love paid for, and love regained. You are a chief character in this story, the one the story's hero gives His life for.

"See what great love the Father has lavished on us, that we should be called children of God! And that is what we are!" (1 John 3:1).

No need for sequins or jewels. No need to work ourselves into exhaustion trying to merit a teacher's recognition or achieve some kind of award.

I cannot fathom a love so great that God would crown me with "glory and honor" (Ps. 8:5). We couldn't deserve such a gift. And yet He offers it just the same.

Take your place on the red carpet, honored one. You're a child of the Most High God. And that's a role worthy of far more than an Oscar.

I have every right to claim all for myself, knowing that an infinite God can give all of Himself to each of His children. He does not distribute Himself that each may have a part, but to each one He gives all of Himself as fully as if there were no others.

—A. W. Tozer, *God's Pursuit of Man*

Day 55

Who Am I?

We spend an incredible amount of time and energy working toward human merit. Although there's nothing wrong with hard work and excellence, it means little when our efforts are expended on temporal things. Consider where you invest your best self. Whose honor do you seek to earn? If you wear Christ, you already wear a crown. Nothing more is required.

Day 56

I Am Satisfied

I am the bread of life. Whoever comes to me will never go hungry, and whoever believes in me will never be thirsty.

John 6:35

Food is his obsession.

He wakes up thinking about food. Goes to sleep thinking about food. And the majority of his conversations and compulsions in the hours between center on the subject of—yes—*food*.

He's eight years old. And there's one simple reason for his food obsession: he knows what it feels like to be hungry.

That's why he eats his dinner in about four minutes flat. That's why he swallows steak whole, without chewing or tasting it. That's why he sneaks into the kitchen when he thinks we're not looking to stuff cookies in his pockets or crackers in his cheeks. When snacks are distributed at church or school, he doesn't take just one like the other children. He grabs five or six, eating as many as he can and stashing extra for later.

Just in case.

Just in case he doesn't have food again for a very long time.

Rest assured we feed our youngest son plenty. Not a day goes by that he doesn't get three squares and a couple of snacks. He does not go without, ever. He eats more than I do. Twice over.

Our son's food obsession began long before he joined our family at four years old. There's a hard history driving his behavior. We know this. But it doesn't make it any easier to wrestle daily with his never-satisfied stomach. No matter how many meals and helpings and snacks we serve up, it's never, ever enough.

You see, hunger doesn't drive him. Fear does.

When you spend the first four years of your life going hungry, you end up a little obsessed with breakfast, lunch, and dinner. It makes sense. Otherwise you might go without.

How about the rest of us? What's our excuse? Most of us don't have the same obsession with food as my eight-year-old son (although, I confess I've been known to tear the house apart looking for a Reese's). Our preoccupation with satisfaction isn't any less dangerous, however.

Consider the woman who works out at the gym hours every week and runs dozens of miles day after day because her body never looks quite trim enough.

Or the man who spends sixty-plus hours a week at the office, to the detriment of his health and family, because he believes the next promotion will finally prove his worth.

And let's not even mention the individual who can't stop shopping and spending and filling her house and closet with the next new thing.

There's nothing wrong with working out, working hard, or dressing nice. That's not the point. Just as food isn't the point for our boy either.

The point is—or rather the question is—what's driving our behavior?

Ultimately, we're searching for something. We want to believe we're sufficiently beautiful, adequately successful. We want satisfaction. That's why we drive ourselves so hard, because we believe if we could just have one more plateful, we'd finally be full.

There's a flaw in that philosophy, however. All our pursuits and passions are merely temporary fixes. That's why today's four-mile run doesn't carry over to tomorrow. And this week's job promotion doesn't mean you won't have to work just as hard for the next one. And that new dress quickly becomes the old dress, buried and forgotten in the back of your closet.

Sure, it feels good for a moment. But an hour or two later, you're hungry all over again. A good breakfast always gives way to a need for lunch.

Yet we don't have to live hungry, obsessing over the next meal. We can finally reach a place where we're no longer afraid of going without. And that happens only when we find a food source that never ends.

To a group of Israelites wandering in the wilderness, God provided the answer. Hungry and afraid, they griped and complained and contemplated returning to their food-deprived slavery. "If only we had died by the LORD's hand in Egypt! There we sat around pots of meat and ate all the food we wanted, but you have brought us out into this desert to starve this entire assembly to death" (Ex. 16:3).

If only I could have what she's having.

If only I could have seconds. Or thirds.

If only . . . if only . . . if only.

God addresses the real need, not their imagined need. They didn't need more food; they needed to trust the one who served it. "I am the LORD your God, who brought you up out of Egypt. Open wide your mouth and I will fill it" (Ps. 81:10).

Not a promise of literal food, although I've known God to provide a meal when times were tight. Rather, a promise of Himself, to satisfy the deeper hunger.

How beautiful—how perfectly beautiful—that Jesus would give Himself a name our starving souls can understand: "I am the bread of life."

The Bread of Life. The only one who can fill what we lack. The only place my boy and I will ever be satisfied.

Go ahead. Run a few miles. Give your best to your job. Buy yourself a new dress or serve up a second helping, if you'd like. But don't, for a second, fool yourself into thinking the pleasure of these lesser plates will last. It's nothing more than a snack, a temporary fix to a forever hunger.

Instead, feast on the Bread of Life, and you will always, always be full.

In an age of information overload, when a vast variety of media delivers news faster than most of us can digest . . . the last thing any of us needs is more information about God. We need the practice of incarnation, by which God saves the lives of those whose intellectual assent has turned as dry as dust, who have run frighteningly low on the bread of life, who are dying to know more God in their bodies. Not more about God. More God.

—Barbara Brown Taylor, *An Altar in the World*

Who Am I?

Jesus calls himself the Bread of Life in John 6, a chapter that also includes the stories of His feeding the five thousand with five loaves and two fish, walking on water during a night of rough seas, and being deserted by many of His followers. I don't think His declaration of His name in the middle of these other stories is an accident. What's the difference between trusting the food and trusting the provider of it? What needs to happen to make that kind of change in a relationship? On a scale of one to five—one being near constant fear of going without to a five being near constant confidence that God will provide—where would you say you stand?

Day 57

I Am Sent

Peace be with you! As the Father has sent me, I am sending you.

—John 20:21

The last thing I planned to do that day was leave my house.

I had a mountain of writing I'd been neglecting and only a small window of time to complete it. I planned to hole up at home, ignore email and phone, and get the job done.

But then the phone rang. And I answered it. Which led to a spontaneous lunch with a friend who needed to talk. It wasn't in my schedule, but I jumped in the car and headed out anyway. I knew what it feels like to need a last-minute listening ear.

But lunch took longer than I planned. Doesn't it always? A sweet afternoon, no doubt about it. But worry over my waiting responsibilities continued to nag me. So I jumped back in my car and pointed it straight toward home. No detours allowed.

Until my phone rang again. And I answered it. It was a work call I'd been waiting for. So I pulled into a coffee shop parking lot where I could talk business without distraction.

Nearly an hour later, I hung up. By now it was well into the late afternoon, and still I hadn't touched my to-do's. Thinking a chai tea latte might energize me, I backed out of my parking space and turned into the drive-through.

Only the drive-through was closed. In the middle of a weekday afternoon. Dear Lord, how was that possible? If I wanted my pick-me-up, I'd have to walk inside.

So once again I parked my car in the parking lot. Frustrated, I glanced at my watch as I walked inside.

That's when I met Lindsey.

Lindsey is a beautiful barista. And when my frustrated self walked up to the crowded counter, she's the one who greeted me with a smile.

"What can I get for you?"

More hours in the day?

"How about a grande chai tea latte?"

"Sure thing." As she pulled out a fresh cup, Lindsey let me know they were now customizing their standard chai. As a result, I could choose my desired sweetness.

In a rare moment of stranger transparency, I mentioned how happy I was about the customization option, because of the fact that multiple surgeries have taken away most of my taste. I can't taste sweet, making added sugar pointless, I told her.

Lindsey paused, sucked in a breath, and whispered, "You're not that woman who wrote that book, are you?"

My turn to pause, inhale. "What book?"

"*Undone*?" I don't think she could've said it any softer.[10]

"Actually, yes." I smiled big. "So nice to meet you!"

And that's when tears filled her eyes. She went on to explain that the week before, she'd heard me tell my story on a radio interview, an ordained moment and message God delivered on a day she desperately needed to hear it.

"That has nothing to do with me," I smiled again. "That's all Him. He loves you."

She nodded in agreement. And then said my showing up in her coffee shop on this particular day was nothing short of a miracle.

If she only knew.

From the moment the day began, God had been orchestrating seemingly errant details to interrupt my well-planned day. Instead of allowing me to hole up at home with my list of to-do's, He sent me out. To a beautiful barista named Lindsey.

A coincidence? No way.

Now, months later, I'm pretty sure all that divine orchestration was for me and not her.

You see, most days I feel a strong urge to hide. To buffer myself from the vulnerable life. There are moments when reality weighs heavy, and I feel overwhelmed with a world that's gone mad.

You know what I mean, don't you? The wars and economic woes and assaults and diseases and accidents. Even beyond all the dramatic evidence of this broken world are the everyday challenges of simply trying to love and live. More often than I care to admit, I want to nestle into the protection of anonymity, hide in a shelter of my own making. Like an ostrich with her head in the sand, I want to close my eyes blind.

And yet, you and I weren't given a light so we could hide it. Our stories weren't written for our own reading any more than the sun is for one person's shining. We've been given stories—broken and beautiful stories—so a broken and beautiful world can see there is a God who's written a story for them too.

Including baristas named Lindsey.

"How, then, can they call on the one they have not believed in? And how can they believe in the one of whom they have not heard? And how can they hear without someone preaching to them? And how can anyone preach unless they are sent? As it is written: 'How beautiful are the feet of those who bring good news!'" (Rom. 10:14–15).

We've been sent, you and I. We're message bearers, storytellers, light givers. None of this can happen, however, if we hide, content to keep our stories to ourselves. There is a great big world waiting to know there is a God who sees and loves them too. Will we leave safety in order to be sent?

The sending is hard, that is true. Both risk and rawness come when we allow God to push us out of hiding and into the light. It means sharing in the suffering of others. Opening yourself to rejection. Facing and feeling the brokenness of a world we once believed was nearly perfect.

And yet I shudder a bit when I think how close I came to staying home that day. How easy it would've been to keep the door locked, stay in my car, refuse to walk inside those coffee shop doors, keep my lips shut about my story.

And I shudder to think how close I came to missing out on God's sweet gift through His sending. Because in offering Lindsey a glimpse of God's love, I got a taste of it for myself too.

Like me, you may wonder why God would choose to send you. I understand. Most days I don't feel up to the task.

And yet as followers of Jesus, we know we are sent. Not on our own merits but on His. Called to carry His name to a world filled with people waiting for a miracle. Ambassadors of the story of all stories to a world of Lindseys searching for it.

Thus, our brokenness can become a gateway to new life.

—Henri J.M. Nouwen, *Bread for the Journey*

Who Am I?

To be an ambassador is to be a representative of another, carrying out the mission of the one doing the sending. It also implies approval, that you've been chosen and sent with the seal of a higher authority. It's not so much about your qualifications as His. Think about that with regard to God's sending of you. How does this change how you perceive and value your life's work?

Day 58

I Am a Light of the World

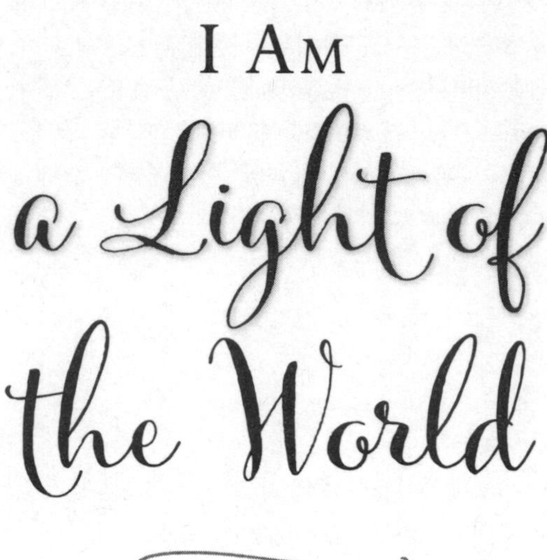

You are the light of the world.
—Matthew 5:14

For the love of all that glitters and shines, lightning bugs can turn an ordinary summer evening into a spectacular show of light.

When I was a young girl growing up in central Illinois, they were the highlight of our summers. It was as if someone sneaked onto our property during the day, stringing Christmas lights high and low. In the pecan and peach trees, through the grass and swing set, along my dad's deck and my mother's rose bushes. Then after daytime flipped off her switch to welcome night, previously invisible strands of lights found their source, lighting up the evening with flashing, twinkling life.

Lightning bugs are irresistible to an eight-year-old child. I'd chase them around my yard, watching as their flashing bodies appeared one moment and disappeared the next. But it wasn't enough to play their game, enjoy their light. I wanted a piece of the action for myself.

That's when Mom's mason jars came out. After poking airholes in the lids, my brother, friends, and I set out to catch as many as possible. The goal? To fill a mason jar with enough light by which to sleep by that night. If a host of lightning bugs could turn the evening sky magical, imagine what they could do to a child's bedroom.

I loved it. My lightning bug jar filled my room with pale green light, my personal lantern. I snuggled deeper under cool sheets and imagined a fairy world filled with flying light.

Still, it wasn't enough. For a neighborhood group of children wanting to create a magical fairy land, we wanted more than mason jars.

Which is when the innocent childhood game of catching lightning bugs turned a bit more sinister. That's when we started removing the lights from the backs of the bugs, a futile and foolish effort to sprinkle our bedroom with nature's nightlight.

Then, at some point, somebody suggested we swallow a few. If a mason jar of light was cool, a little girl filled with lightning bugs was certain to become a human lantern. I wouldn't *have* a light; I'd *be* a light.

Gulp!

But swallowing a lightning bug never made a well-intentioned child shine. And removing the lights from our buggy friends only caused the glow to go out. Even the mason jars filled with living, breathing lightning bugs eventually dimmed.

It didn't take us long to learn that lightning bugs weren't meant to light a child's room.

They were made to light their world.

"You're here to be light, bringing out the God-colors in the world. God is not a secret to be kept. We're going public with this, as public as a city on a hill. If I make you light-bearers, you don't think I'm going to hide you under a bucket, do you? I'm putting you on a light stand.

Day 58

Now that I've put you there on a hilltop, on a light stand—shine! Keep open house; be generous with your lives. By opening up to others, you'll prompt people to open up with God, this generous Father in heaven" (Matt. 5:14–16 MSG).

Our love of light is obvious. We deck out everything from our homes—inside and out—to our clothes to our cars with accessories that glitter. Move past the material, though, and you'll still see our near-desperation to be shining people. We grasp for attention, trying to woo the world with our twinkling selves. Whether it's our social media addiction or our tendency to self-promote or our chronic dysfunction in relationships, we're trapped in a world we were never created to endure.

But like bugs in a jar, we can't hope to shine if we're captive to a lesser way of life. The only way to shine brightly is to take flight, to be fully and freely who we were made to be.

People so filled with the Light of the World that they can't help but shine.

Jesus said, "I am the light of the world. Whoever follows me will never walk in darkness, but will have the light of life" (John 8:12). Jesus is the light that shines brighter than all others. But you can't watch Him from a distance, pick and choose the pieces you want, or put Him in a jar.

You must swallow Him, all of Him. If you want to shine, Jesus must become as much a part of you as your blue eyes or your brown hair. When you do, when you decide to make Jesus a part of your life in every way, you will shine from the inside out. It's transforming, this Jesus-swallowing. Both for you and those around you.

And it's a light that does not dim or fade, no matter how dark the darkness becomes. The blacker the night, the brighter the shine.

Shine, my friends, shine. You have the Light of Life living in you, filling you with a glory you couldn't capture if you tried. Receive His light. And then, shine bright.

In a futile attempt to erase our past, we deprive the community of our healing gift. If we conceal our wounds out of fear and shame, our inner darkness can neither be illuminated nor become a light for others.

—Brennan Manning, *Abba's Child*

Who Am I?

It's incredible to think that Jesus called us the "light of the world." A pretty significant title for ordinary, flawed humankind. And yet those who know Jesus have been transformed, as much as a sunrise transforms the night. Even better, Jesus' light never sets nor fades. Imagine what would happen if all of these individual Jesus lights came together to shine. Just as a string of lights illuminates far more than a single bulb can, the church can infiltrate the darkness of this world. How can you, a single member of this greater family, shine your light?

Day 59

I Am Enough

It is not the healthy who need a doctor, but the sick. . . .
for I have not come to call the righteous, but sinners.
—Matthew 9:12–13

It is not an easy thing to both exit and reenter this world on the same day. And I believe it's even worse when you reenter it as a different person.

This is what happened in the early stages of writing this book. I initially thought the timing to be terrible. I had a book to write—a book on identity and making peace, once and for all, with who we truly are. I now wonder if the timing was divine.

I should note I did not experience actual death. No reincarnation or resurrection. And no Lazarus-sized miracles, in spite of my repeated, face-on-the-floor prayers. But I did endure a very real death. A death I would've done just about anything to avoid.

After the third cancer diagnosis and brutal surgery that included the removal of two-thirds of my tongue, multiple incisions, skin grafts, and major reconstruction, I arose from anesthesic bliss to discover a woman I no longer recognized. I went to sleep whole and woke up broken.

Before the doctor injected happy-sleepy serum into my veins, I was able to talk and swallow and sing and kiss my husband and eat a four-course gourmet meal.

Nine hours later, I woke up in a cold and hollow hospital room unable to do any of those things.

In that moment, and countless times in the days, weeks, and months that followed, I discovered, to my deep pain, that I was not—nor will ever be—the woman I was before. Like watching a horror movie looping its most terrifying scene, I was forced to face the brutal truth again and again.

Permanent physical disability, they call it. Eating is now an exercise that takes at least twice as long as it used to. Even worse, the exercise comes with no reward. I taste little of what I work so hard to chew and swallow. I can speak, but only with great effort, imperfect enunciation, and a gravelly voice I don't recognize. And then there's the constant choking, a body scissored with scars, and chronic discomfort.

Permanent disability? Yes, you could say that.

For a woman who long prided herself on living a well-ordered life, it's not an easy thing to accept a body that won't fall into line. For months I raged against it, grieved the loss with tears that wouldn't stop.

Until I started to see that wrestling with my physical self was simply mirroring a deeper, inward struggle.

For too long I'd lived a slave to my performance. In school. In parenting. In marriage. In career. In housekeeping. In faith. In spite of my near-constant exhaustion, I could never allow myself to rest. There were always flaws that needed fixing, attitudes that needed adjusting, countertops that required cleaning, and relationships that needed mending. Everywhere I looked I saw a disability that needed healing. And so I rolled up my emotional sleeves and determined to *be better.*

But in all that striving, I failed to realize two important truths, the first truth being that I'd had a permanent disability long before surgery. In spite of all my good intentions and hard efforts, I have always been and always will be *human*. That means I'm complicated, flawed, sinful.

Day 59

No amount of hard work will heal my brokenness. Any attempts to fix myself will merely lead to further disappointment and insecurity.

The second truth I realized is this: I am enough. I don't need to wipe up all my messes and fix all my flaws. I'm not required to get my act together or put on a good show. My identity has nothing to do with me. Instead, I am loved by someone who has loved me from the beginning of time, even knowing the ways I'd end up disfigured and disabled.

Romans 5:6–8 says this: "Christ arrives right on time to make this happen. He didn't, and doesn't, wait for us to get ready. He presented himself for this sacrificial death when we were far too weak and rebellious to do anything to get ourselves ready. And even if we hadn't been so weak, we wouldn't have known what to do anyway. We can understand someone dying for a person worth dying for, and we can understand how someone good and noble could inspire us to selfless sacrifice. But God put his love on the line for us by offering his Son in sacrificial death while we were of no use whatever to him" (MSG).

No use whatever. He didn't choose and love and save because you and I were useful. He didn't throw His heart at the world because we'd eventually earn back His exorbitant cost.

He did it simply for love. He sees beyond our failures and flaws, our successes and showing off. He knows our fickle hearts and our inability to keep our promises. And yet He promises to stay true to us. Forever. That means, disabled or not, I'm enough. You're enough. Exactly as we are. Because the miracle never hinged on us in the first place.

That is the one thing I long for you to take away from these sixty days together.

You are not your mistakes. Nor are you your successes.

You are not your accusers' criticisms. Nor are you your fans' affirmations.

You are not your character flaws or your character strengths.

You are because He is.

Created. Saved. Worth coming back for.

And enough.

In the concentration camp I lived near a crematorium for months. I was living in the shadow of death . . . When you face eternity, and that was what was happening to me, you see everything so clearly. Here I was weak and sinful, and there was the Devil, much stronger than me, much, much stronger than me. But there was Jesus, much, much stronger than the Devil. And together with Him, I was more than a conqueror.

—Corrie ten Boom, *I Stand at the Door and Knock*

Who Am I?

Most of us feel lacking in some regard. Lacking intelligence, beauty, resources, personality, wit, relationships, talents. You name it, we want more of it. Consider your nagging list of less-than's. In a journal or in the margin of this book, write them down. But for heaven's sake, don't stop there. After you're done, write one giant, bold-print word right over the top: ENOUGH.

Day 60

I Am Going Home

At that time I will gather you; at that time I will bring you home.

—Zephaniah 3:20

I happen to think Dorothy and Glinda the good witch were onto something. There is, in fact, no place like home.

No vacation beach or resort or chalet, regardless of the expense and glamour, can match the sweet comfort of home. As much as I enjoy an escape from ordinary life and need one from time to time, there's nothing quite as sweet as coming home again.

The feel of my favorite coffee mug in hand. The warmth and snuggle of my king-sized down comforter. The smell of my favorite lavender candle and the feel of a fluffy bath towel. The mocking bird who sings to me while I sip my coffee on the deck in the early morning. The beloved faces of husband and children in the family portrait hanging near the front door.

Home.

I wonder if that's the reason for my dad's peace in the final weeks and days of his life. He knew he was going home.

There were tears too, of course. You can't say goodbye to those you love without feeling a pang of loss. But his awareness of and confidence in what was to come trumped even his pain. I saw it in the ease of his smile, in the way he sought to comfort and reassure us, in his ability to sleep deeply and soundly, without anxiety or fear.

He knew. Life waited on the other side of death.

Perhaps this was most clearly seen on his final Saturday afternoon, three short days before he slipped away from us. We knew time was short. And so we circled his hospice-delivered bed to do church. My mom, his wife of forty-six years. My brother, sister-in-law, and nieces. My husband and children. We gathered around the man whose choosing Jesus at twenty-seven years old resulted in a family full of faith.

Over the previous forty-eight hours, he'd stopped responding to nearly all interactions. We made repeated efforts to engage him, talk with him. Still, he slept, lost to an in-between place. Although we prayed otherwise, I doubted he comprehended our Saturday afternoon church service.

One person shared the story of Jesus washing the disciples' feet, because everyone who knew Dad knew he spent a lifetime washing feet. Another read Psalm 112, words that perfectly describe this man: "They will have no fear of bad news; their hearts are steadfast, trusting in the LORD" (v. 7). We shared communion. We prayed.

Holding his hand, kissing his forehead, we took turns telling him how he'd led us, taught us, and inspired us to love God and others without restraint. And to run the race with passion to the very end.

Then we played a single worship song: Matt Redman's "10,000 Reasons." Standing around his bed, we sang loud and strong, the tears falling like a flood. In spite of the countless times we'd sung the same song at church, this time was different. The words came alive. We now understood their truth. A man was slipping through our fingers, but heaven was not.

But Dad wasn't to be outdone. He still had breath left. And so this man who had chosen Jesus and spent his life in worship opened his mouth and started to sing, even in death:

Day 60

And on that day when my strength is failing
The end draws near and my time has come
Still my soul will sing Your praise unending
Ten thousand years and then forevermore!
Bless the Lord, O my soul
O my soul
Worship His holy name
Sing like never before
O my soul
I'll worship Your holy name.

At the last note, with wife and children in hushed silence, he simply said, "Amen. Hallelujah."

Those were the last words he ever spoke. With a sigh, he fell back into deep, peace-filled sleep. Seventy-two hours later, he was gone.

Even now, more than a year later, I hear the echo of his singing. My dad gave voice to what has stirred in my soul from the moment of my birth: a longing for something more.

It's as if every cell knows there is something far grander and worthier than what this temporary life offers. And I feel a chronic, unresolved longing, as if I'm waiting.

Because I am. And so are you. As beautiful and rich as this life can be, it's merely a short-term vacation. A trip to a place with fresh sights and sounds and adventures. But a temporary destination. We are living out of suitcases, grateful for the gift, but knowing it cannot compare with home.

On the days when the story of my life is hard, when the sweetness is swallowed by the reality of pain and brokenness, this thought—this *hope*—is the only thing that gets me through.

Whatever your story, whatever tornado has ripped through your life and landed you in a place with which you're not familiar, there is one who knows how to get you back home.

A Savior.

A God With Us who promised to come for us.

"Behold, I am coming soon!" He says.

And so we wait, eyes to the sky, searching and hoping that maybe today—today!—will be the day when this life slips through our fingers, and the next life—our real life—begins.

Home.

Amen, hallelujah. Praise the Lord.

Faith is what makes life bearable, with all its tragedies and ambiguities and sudden startling joys. Surely it wasn't reasonable of the Lord of the Universe to come and walk this earth with us and love us enough to die for us and then show us everlasting life? We will all grow old, and sooner or later we will die, like the old trees in the orchard. But we have been promised that this is not the end. We have been promised life.

—Madeleine L'Engle, *Walking on Water*

Who Am I?

Western culture is unique in the fact that we spend a significant amount of time and energy avoiding the subject of death. From what we eat to the way we talk, we work hard to prevent it, deny it, skirt around it. And yet the inevitability of death is what fuels the quality of life. Psalm 32:7 says, "You are my hiding place." God alone is our home. When we embrace this, when we face the limits of this life and the reality of death, we finally discover a security of identity, a tranquility of soul. No fear in life or death. No worry over what may or may not come. Because this is only the barest hint of the glory awaiting us.

NOTES

1. Timothy Keller, *The Reason for God: Belief in an Age of Skepticism* (New York: Riverhead, 2008), 171.
2. John Piper, John Piper Messages Podcast, August 31, 2014, based on an article on *Desiring God*, https://itunes.apple.com/us/podcast/john-piper-messages-audio/id196050704?mt=2&i=318863842.
3. Spiros Zodhiates, ThD, executive editor, *Hebrew-Greek Key Word Study Bible* (Chattanooga, TN: AMG Publishers, 1996), #3231, 1643.
4. *Beauty At Any Cost: A YWCA Report on the Consequences of America's Beauty Obsession on Women and Girls*, August 2008, http://www.ywca.org/atf/cf/%7B711d5519-9e3c-4362-b753-ad138b5d352c%7D/BEAUTY-AT-ANY-COST.PDF.
5. Zodhiates, *Hebrew-Greek Key Word Study Bible*, #2876, 1516.
6. Quoted in Franklin Graham and Donna Lee Toney, *Billy Graham in Quotes*.
7. Elizabeth Hernandez, "Why Thousands of Denver Trees Are Dying This Year," *Denver Post*, September 14, 2015, http://www.denverpost.com/2015/09/14/why-thousands-of-denver-area-trees-are-dying-this-year/.
8. Becky Johnson and Rachel Randolph, *Nourished: A Search for Health, Happiness and a Full Night's Sleep* (Grand Rapids, MI: Zondervan, 2015), 246.
9. Matthew Henry, *Matthew Henry Commentary on the Whole Bible* (1706).
10. Michele Cushatt, *Undone: A Story of Making Peace with an Unexpected Life* (Grand Rapids, MI: Zondervan, 2015).

Undone

A Story of Making Peace with an Unexpected Life

Michele Cushatt

Sometimes life's greatest beauty shows up in life's greatest chaos. Michele Cushatt wanted a well-ordered life. Peaceful, predictable, and happy. A life she could control.

She never expected a devastating divorce and single-motherhood. Or a second marriage marred by the challenges of a blended family.

Undaunted, Michele worked hard to put her upside-down life back in order. Until, at the age of thirty-nine, she received a cancer diagnosis. And eight months later, she opened her near-empty-nest home to three little ones in crisis. The resulting chaos proved far more than she could contain.

The secret to peace is finding eyes to see.

Undone is Michele's story of discovery, of learning that all her attempts to control her life were robbing her of its vibrancy, and that faith in the midst of the unknown is the only real kind of faith at all. It is her call for each of us to relinquish perfection and embrace what is. To lean in. Because right here, right now, in your own unfinished story with its missteps and misfortunes, there is peace. And there is Presence. Because sometimes life's best stories are written right in the middle of the mess.

Available in stores and online!

I Am
Memory Verse Downloads

Michele Cushatt

Now you can take the messages of *I Am* wherever you go! Michele has created sixty memory verse cards—one for each chapter of the book. You can download them for free by visiting michelecushatt.com/IAmBook.

Michele Cushatt

For more information on Michele, please visit her website, michelecushatt.com. There you will find her blog, speaking calendar, podcasts, and all her latest news and information.

For more information on booking Michele to speak at your next event, please visit michelecushatt.com or email joyg@thefrontlinegroup.com.